OECD-FAO Guidance for Responsible Agricultural Supply Chains

This document and any map included herein are without prejudice to the status of or sovereignty over any territory, to the delimitation of international frontiers and boundaries and to the name of any territory, city or area. The names of countries and territories used in this joint publication follow the practice of the FAO.

Please cite this publication as:
OECD/FAO (2016), OECD-FAO *Guidance for Responsible Agricultural Supply Chains*, OECD Publishing, Paris.
http://dx.doi.org/10.1787/9789264251052-en

ISBN 978-92-64-25095-6 (print)
ISBN 978-92-64-25105-2 (PDF)

FAO :
ISBN 978-92-5-109395-5 (print and PDF)

The statistical data for Israel are supplied by and under the responsibility of the relevant Israeli authorities. The use of such data by the OECD is without prejudice to the status of the Golan Heights, East Jerusalem and Israeli settlements in the West Bank under the terms of international law.

Photo credits: Cover © pink_cotton_candy/iStock/Thinkstock.com

Corrigenda to OECD publications may be found on line at: *www.oecd.org/about/publishing/corrigenda.htm*.

Foreword

The OECD-FAO Guidance for Responsible Agricultural Supply Chains (the Guidance) has been developed to help enterprises observe existing standards for responsible business conduct along agricultural supply chains. These standards include the OECD Guidelines for Multinational Enterprises, the Principles for Responsible Investment in Agriculture and Food Systems, and the Voluntary Guidelines on the Responsible Governance of Tenure of Land, Fisheries and Forests in the Context of National Food Security. Observing these standards helps enterprises mitigate their adverse impacts and contribute to sustainable development.

The Guidance targets all enterprises operating along agricultural supply chains, including domestic and foreign, private and public, small, medium and large-scale enterprises. It covers agricultural upstream and downstream sectors from input supply to production, post-harvest handling, processing, transportation, marketing, distribution and retailing. Several areas of risk arising along agricultural supply chains are addressed: human right, labour rights, health and safety, food security and nutrition, tenure rights over and access to natural resources, animal welfare, environmental protection and sustainable use of natural resources, governance, and technology and innovation.

The Guidance comprises four sections:

- *a model enterprise policy outlining the standards that enterprises should observe to build responsible agricultural supply chains*
- *a framework for risk-based due diligence describing the five steps that enterprises should follow to identify, assess, mitigate and account for how they address the adverse impacts of their activities*
- *a description of the major risks faced by enterprises and the measures to mitigate these risks*
- *guidance for engaging with indigenous peoples.*

The Guidance was developed by OECD and FAO through a two-year multi-stakeholder process. It was approved by the OECD Investment Committee, the OECD Committee for Agriculture, and the Cabinet of FAO Director-General. A Recommendation on the Guidance was adopted by the OECD Council on 13 July 2016. While not legally binding, the Recommendation reflects the common position and political commitment of OECD members and non-member adherents.

The OECD has also developed tailored guidance to help enterprises build responsible supply chains in other sectors, specifically: extractives, and particularly minerals from conflict-affected and high-risk areas; garment and footwear; and finance.

Table of contents

Table

Figures

Boxes

Follow OECD Publications on:

 http://twitter.com/OECD_Pubs

 http://www.facebook.com/OECDPublications

 http://www.linkedin.com/groups/OECD-Publications-4645871

 http://www.youtube.com/oecdilibrary

http://www.oecd.org/oecddirect/

Follow FAO on:

Food and Agriculture Organization of the United Nations

 twitter.com/FAOstatistics
twitter.com/FAOKnowledge
twitter.com/FAOnews

 www.facebook.com/UNFAO

 www.linkedin.com/company/fao

 plus.google.com/+UNFAO

 www.instagram.com/unfao

 www.youtube.com/user/FAOoftheUN

Acronyms and abbreviations

CAO	Compliance Advisor Ombudsman of IFC and MIGA
CBD	Convention on Biological Diversity
CEDAW	Convention on the Elimination of All Forms of Discrimination Against Women
CFS	Committee on World Food Security
CFS-RAI	Principles for Responsible Investment in Agriculture and Food Systems of the Committee on World Food Security
CSR	Corporate Social Responsibility
EIA	Environmental Impact Assessment
ESHRIA	Environmental, Social and Human Rights Impact Assessment
EU	European Union
FAO	Food and Agriculture Organization of the United Nations
FDI	Foreign Direct Investment
FPIC	Free, Prior and Informed Consent
ICESCR	International Covenant on Economic, Social and Cultural Rights
IFAD	International Fund for Agricultural Development
IFC	International Finance Corporation
IFPRI	International Food Policy Research Institute
ILO	International Labour Organization

ITPGR	International Treaty on Plant Genetic Resources for Food and Agriculture
MIGA	Multilateral Investment Guarantee Agency
MNE	Multinational Enterprise
NCP	National Contact Point
NGO	Non-governmental Organisation
OECD	Organisation for Economic Co-operation and Development
OIE	World Organization for Animal Health
PRAI	Principles for Responsible Agricultural Investment that respects rights, livelihoods and resources developed by FAO, International Fund for Agricultural Development (IFAD), United Nations Conference on Trade and Development (UNCTAD) and World Bank
RBC	Responsible Business Conduct
VGGT	Voluntary Guidelines on the Responsible Governance of Tenure of Land, Fisheries and Forests in the Context of National Food Security
UN	United Nations
UNCTAD	United Nations Conference on Trade and Development
US	United States
USD	United States Dollar
WB	World Bank
WHO	World Health Organization

Preface

The OECD-FAO Guidance for Responsible Agricultural Supply Chains responds to a critical need for practical guidance on responsible business conduct for enterprises operating in the agricultural sector. Investments in agriculture have grown in recent years and are expected to continue to grow as the sector expands to meet increasing demand. As investments in the sector have grown, so too has the awareness that they need to be responsible. Standards of responsible business conduct along agricultural supply chains are essential to ensure that the benefits are widespread and that agriculture continues to fulfil its multiple functions, including food security, poverty reduction, and economic growth.

The OECD-FAO Guidance was developed over the period October 2013 to September 2015 under the guidance of a multi-stakeholder Advisory Group, including representatives from OECD and non-OECD members, the private sector, and civil society. The Advisory Group is chaired by David Hegwood, Chief of Global Engagement and Strategy, Bureau for Food Security at USAID. The three Vice Chairs represent the various stakeholder groups: Mella Frewen, Director General of FoodDrink Europe; Bernd Schanzenbaecher, Founder and Managing Partner of EBG Capital; and Kris Genovese, Senior Researcher at the Centre for Research on Multinational Corporations (SOMO) and Co-Coordinator of OECD Watch.

In the course of its work, the Advisory Group held three in-person meetings and three consultations via conference call. It held its first meeting on 16 October 2013 and subsequent meetings on 26 June 2014 and 16 March 2015. It also held a joint meeting with the Advisory Group on Meaningful Stakeholder Engagement in the Extractive Sector on 18 June 2015 to discuss free, prior and informed consent. Conference calls were organised on 10 February 2014, 28 May 2014 and 7 January 2015. An online public consultation was held in January and February 2015 to receive comments from a wider range of stakeholders on the draft Guidance.

The OECD-FAO Guidance also benefitted from the conclusions of the Global Forum on Responsible Business Conduct held in 2014 and 2015. On 27 June 2014, a special session on responsible agricultural supply chains identified the major risks faced by enterprises when investing in agricultural supply chains and discussed the measures that governments and enterprises could take to mitigate such risks and ensure that agricultural investment benefits home and host countries as well as investors. On 19 June 2015, a panel discussion explored the roles and responsibilities of various types of enterprises operating along agricultural supply chains and the ways they could collaborate to carry out due diligence.

The diversity of perspectives represented within the Advisory Group contributed to the development of a guidance document that emphasises respect for the rights of all stakeholders adversely impacted by operations along agricultural supply chains, defines the roles and responsibilities of enterprises operating along these supply chains, and proposes practical approaches to mitigate the risks faced by enterprises. We are confident this OECD-FAO Guidance will be a useful tool to guide enterprises in conducting their due diligence. We believe it will also promote the observance of the existing standards that were considered in its development.

David Hegwood

Chair of the Multi-stakeholder Advisory Group
and Chief, Global Engagement and Strategy, Bureau for Food Security, USAID

Recommendation of the Council on the OECD-FAO Guidance for Responsible Agricultural Supply Chains

13 July 2016

THE COUNCIL,

HAVING REGARD to Article 5 b) of the Convention on the Organisation for Economic Co-operation and Development of 14 December 1960;

HAVING REGARD to the Declaration on International Investment and Multinational Enterprises [C(76)99/FINAL], the Decision of the Council on the OECD Guidelines for Multinational Enterprises [C(2000)96/FINAL as amended by C/MIN(2011)11/FINAL] (hereafter the "Decision on the Guidelines"), the Convention on Combating Bribery of Foreign Public Officials in International Business Transactions, the Recommendation of the Council on Due Diligence Guidance for Responsible Supply Chains of Minerals from Conflict-Affected and High-Risk Areas [C/MIN(2011)12/FINAL as amended by C(2012)93], and the Recommendation of the Council on the Policy Framework for Investment [C(2015)56/REV1];

RECALLING that the common aim of governments recommending the observance of the Guidelines for Multinational Enterprises (hereafter the "Guidelines") is to promote responsible business conduct;

RECALLING FURTHER that the Decision on the Guidelines provides that the Investment Committee shall, in co-operation with National Contact Points, pursue a proactive agenda in collaboration with stakeholders to promote the effective observance by enterprises of the principles and standards contained in the Guidelines with respect to particular products, regions, sectors or industries;

CONSIDERING the efforts of the international community, in particular the Committee on World Food Security and the Food and Agriculture Organization of the United Nations (FAO), to promote responsible investment in agriculture and food systems and the responsible governance of tenure of land, fisheries and forests;

RECOGNISING that building responsible agricultural supply chains is critical to sustainable development;

RECOGNISING that governments, enterprises, civil society organisations and international organisations can draw on their respective competences and roles to build responsible agricultural supply chains that benefit society at large;

NOTING that due diligence is an on-going, proactive and reactive process through which enterprises can ensure that they observe government-backed standards for responsible agricultural supply chains related to human rights, labour rights, health and safety, food security and nutrition, tenure rights, animal welfare, environmental protection and the use of natural resources, governance and technology and innovation;

HAVING REGARD to the OECD-FAO Guidance for Responsible Agricultural Supply Chains [C(2016)83/ADD1] (hereafter "the Guidance"), that may be modified as appropriate by the Investment Committee and the Committee for Agriculture in co-operation with the FAO;

NOTING that this Guidance proposes a model enterprise policy outlining the content of existing standards for responsible agricultural supply chains and a five-step framework for due diligence describing the steps that enterprises should follow to identify, assess, mitigate and account for how they address the actual and potential adverse impacts associated with their activities or business relationships;

On the proposal of the Investment Committee and the Committee for Agriculture:

I. **RECOMMENDS** that Members and non-Members adhering to this Recommendation (hereafter the "Adherents") and, where relevant, their National Contact Points to the Guidelines (hereafter the "NCPs"), actively promote the use of the Guidance by enterprises operating in or from their territories with the aim of ensuring that they observe internationally agreed standards of responsible business conduct along agricultural supply chains in order to prevent the adverse impacts of their activities and contribute to sustainable development, and in particular poverty reduction, food security and gender equality;

II. **RECOMMENDS**, in particular, that Adherents take measures to actively support the adoption of the model enterprise policy by enterprises operating in or from their territories and the integration into corporate management systems of the five-step framework for risk-based due diligence along agricultural supply chains set out in the Guidance;

III. **RECOMMENDS** that Adherents and where relevant their NCPs, with the support of the OECD Secretariat including through its activities with the United Nations and international development organisations, ensure the widest possible dissemination of the Guidance and its active use by various stakeholders, including on-farm, downstream and upstream enterprises, affected communities and civil society organisations, and regularly report to the Investment Committee and the Committee for Agriculture on any dissemination and implementation activities;

IV. **INVITES** Adherents and the Secretary-General to disseminate this Recommendation;

V. **INVITES** non-Adherents to take due account of and adhere to the present Recommendation;

VI. **INSTRUCTS** the Investment Committee and the Committee for Agriculture to monitor the implementation of the Recommendation and to report to Council no later than five years following its adoption and as appropriate thereafter.

1. Introduction

Background

The agricultural sector,[1] with more than 570 million farms in the world, should continue attracting further investment. This is notably the case for South Asia and Sub-Saharan Africa where agricultural capital stock per worker is relatively low at USD 1 700 and USD 2 200 respectively, compared to USD 16 500 in Latin America and the Caribbean and USD 19 000 in Europe and Central Asia (FAO, 2012 and 2014). In the coming decade, prices for agricultural products are projected to remain at a higher level than in the years preceding the 2007-08 price spike as the demand for food increases driven by growing populations, higher incomes, and changing diets. The demand for non-food agricultural products is also increasing (OECD/FAO, 2015).

Enterprises operating along agricultural supply chains can make a significant contribution to sustainable development by creating employment and bringing expertise, technology and financing capacities for increasing agricultural production sustainably and upgrading in supply chains. This can enhance food and nutritional security and help achieve the development goals of the host country. Internationally agreed principles of responsible business conduct (RBC)[2] aim to ensure that enterprises contribute to sustainable development. They are already used by a significant number of enterprises. The risks of not observing these principles may be exacerbated as new actors, such as institutional investors, are increasingly involved in agricultural supply chains and as a growing number of investors target new markets, including in countries with weak governance frameworks.

Providing guidance to enterprises involved in agricultural supply chains on how to observe existing RBC standards[3] is essential to prevent adverse impacts and ensure that agricultural investments benefit enterprises,[4] governments and communities and contribute to sustainable development, and in particular poverty reduction, food security and gender equality. The range of enterprises targeted by this Guidance for Responsible Agricultural Supply Chains (hereafter "the Guidance") includes enterprises directly involved in agricultural production, such as small-scale producers, as well as other actors involved through business relationships,[5] such as investment funds, sovereign wealth funds or banks.[6]

Purpose

The Guidance intends to help enterprises observe existing standards for RBC along agricultural supply chains,[7] including the OECD Guidelines for Multinational Enterprises (OECD Guidelines). It aims to prevent risks of adverse environmental, social and human rights impacts, providing a potentially useful complement to the work of the National Contact Points (NCPs) which are tasked with furthering the effectiveness of the OECD Guidelines (see Box 1.1). It can help governments, particularly NCPs, in their efforts to promote the OECD Guidelines and in clarifying existing standards in the agricultural sector.

The Guidance refers to existing standards to help enterprises observe them and undertake risk-based due diligence. It only refers to the parts of the OECD Guidelines and other standards that are most relevant to agricultural supply chains and does not aim to substitute them. Enterprises should thus refer directly to each of these standards before making any claims regarding their observance. Not all adherents to the Declaration on International Investment and Multinational Enterprises, of which the OECD Guidelines form an integral part, or members of the FAO endorse the standards considered in this Guidance.

Scope

The Guidance considers existing standards that are relevant for responsible business conduct along agricultural supply chains, including:

- The OECD Guidelines for Multinational Enterprises (OECD Guidelines)
- The Principles for Responsible Investment in Agriculture and Food Systems of the Committee on World Food Security (CFS-RAI Principles)
- The Voluntary Guidelines on the Responsible Governance of Tenure of Land, Fisheries and Forests in the Context of National Food Security of the Committee on World Food Security (VGGT)
- The Principles for Responsible Agricultural Investment that Respects Rights, Livelihoods and Resources developed by FAO, International Fund for Agricultural Development (IFAD), UN Conference on Trade and Development (UNCTAD) and the World Bank (PRAI)
- The Guiding Principles on Business and Human Rights [Implementing the UN 'Protect, Respect and Remedy' Framework] (UN Guiding Principles)
- The International Labour Organization Tripartite Declaration of Principles concerning Multinational Enterprises and Social Policy (ILO MNE Declaration)
- The Convention on Biological Diversity (CBD), including the Akwé: Kon Voluntary Guidelines
- The Convention on Access to Information, Public Participation in Decision-Making and Access to Justice in Environmental Matters of the UN Economic Commission for Europe (Aarhus Convention).

The above standards meet the following three criteria established by the Advisory Group:[8] they have been negotiated and/or endorsed through an inter-governmental process; they are relevant to agricultural supply chains; and they target in particular the business/investor community. The four key standards considered in this Guidance are further described in Box 1.1. The Guidance also considers the following standards that do not meet these criteria but that are being widely used to the extent that they are consistent with the standards listed above:

- The International Finance Corporation's Performance Standards
- The Principles of the UN Global Compact.

Additional instruments, such as UN human rights treaties, are also referred to when they are relevant for the implementation of the above standards. In addition, enterprises may find it useful to refer to other standards that have not been considered in this Guidance as well to more specific tools and guidance: a list of those is available online.[9]

Box 1.1. **Description of the key standards considered in the Guidance**

OECD Guidelines for Multinational Enterprises *(OECD Guidelines)*: The OECD Guidelines are one of four parts of the 1976 OECD Declaration on International Investment and Multinational Enterprises, by which Adherents commit to provide an open and transparent international investment environment and to encourage the positive contribution of multinational enterprises (MNEs) to economic and social progress. There are currently 46 Adherents to the Declaration - 34 OECD and 12 non-OECD economies.[1] The OECD Guidelines have been revised several times, most recently in 2011. They are the most comprehensive set of government-backed recommendations on what constitutes RBC. They cover nine major areas of RBC: information disclosure, human rights, employment and industrial relations, environment, bribery and corruption, consumer interests, science and technology, competition, and taxation. They are addressed by governments to MNEs operating in and from the Adherents. Each Adherent must set up a NCP to further the effectiveness of the Guidelines by undertaking promotional activities, handling inquiries, and contributing to the resolution of issues that arise relating to the implementation of the Guidelines in specific instances. The Guidelines are the first international instrument to integrate the corporate responsibility to respect human rights as set out in the UN Guiding Principles and to incorporate risk-based due diligence into major areas of business ethics related to adverse impacts.[2]

Principles for Responsible Investment in Agriculture and Food Systems *(CFS-RAI Principles)*: The principles were developed through intergovernmental negotiations led by the Committee on World Food Security (CFS) from 2012 to 2014 and involved civil society organisations, private sector, academics, researchers, and international organisations. They were endorsed by the CFS on 15 October 2014 at its 41st session. They are voluntary and non-binding and address all types of investment in agriculture and food systems. They contain ten core principles related to: food security and nutrition; sustainable and inclusive economic development and poverty eradication; gender equality and women's empowerment; youth; tenure of land, fisheries, and forests and access to water; sustainable management of natural resources; cultural heritage, traditional knowledge, diversity and innovation; safe and healthy agriculture; inclusive and transparent governance structures, processes, and grievance mechanisms; impacts and accountability. An additional section describes the roles and responsibilities of stakeholders.

Voluntary Guidelines on the Responsible Governance of Tenure of Land, Fisheries and Forests in the Context of National Food Security *(VGGT)*: The VGGT are the first global guidelines on the governance of tenure. They were developed through intergovernmental negotiations led by the CFS and also involved civil society organisations, the private sector, academics and researchers, and international organisations. They were endorsed by the CFS at its 38th (Special) Session on 11 May 2012. The VGGT have received global recognition and their implementation has been encouraged by the G20 and in the Rio +20 Declaration. On 21 December 2012, the UN General Assembly: welcomed the outcome of the 38th (Special) Session of CFS which endorsed the VGGT; encouraged countries to give due consideration to their implementation; and requested relevant UN entities to ensure their speedy distribution and promotion.[3] These Guidelines provide a reference framework to improve the governance of tenure of land, fisheries and forests that supports food security and contributes to the global and national efforts towards the eradication of hunger and poverty. Recognising the central role of land in development, they promote secure tenure rights and equitable access to land, fisheries and forests. They set out principles and internationally accepted practices that may guide the preparation and implementation of policies and laws related to tenure governance. These Guidelines build on and support the *Voluntary Guidelines to Support the Progressive Realization of the Right to Adequate Food in the Context of National Food Security,* which were adopted by the FAO Council in November 2004.

Box 1.1. **Description of the key standards considered in the Guidance** *(cont.)*

Principles for Responsible Agricultural Investment that Respects Rights, Livelihoods and Resources *(PRAI)*: The Inter-Agency Working Group (IAWG) composed of IFAD, FAO, UNCTAD and World Bank held a roundtable during the UN General Assembly in September 2009 on 'Promoting Responsible International Investment in Agriculture' to present the seven principles and subsequently published a synoptic version in February 2010. The seven principles focus on: land and resource rights; food security; transparency, good governance and the enabling environment; consultation and participation; responsible agro-enterprise investing; social sustainability; and environmental sustainability.[4] At its Seoul Summit in November 2010, the G20 encouraged 'all countries and companies to uphold the Principles for Responsible Agricultural Investment' as part of its multi-year action plan on development. The IAWG submitted a report on the PRAI and a Plan of Action on Options for Promoting Responsible Investment in Agriculture to the G20 in 2011 and the G8 in 2012.[5] The G20 agreed with a twin track approach as the way forward to both pilot the PRAI and use the lessons learned to inform various consultation processes. In October 2012, the IAWG submitted a progress report on its action plan with particular reference to the field-testing of the PRAI with host countries and enterprises.[6] Recently, the 2013 Saint Petersburg Accountability Report on G20 Development Commitments 'welcomed the progress of the pilot projects field-testing the PRAIs in some African and South-East Asian countries'.

1. As of February 2016, these are Argentina, Brazil, Colombia, Costa Rica, Egypt, Jordan, Latvia, Lithuania, Morocco, Peru, Romania, and Tunisia.
2. Due diligence applies to all the chapters of the Guidelines, except science and technology, competition and taxation.
3. *www.un.org/News/Press/docs//2012/ga11332.doc.htm*.
4. The text of the PRAI can be downloaded at *www.responsibleagroinvestment.org*.
5. Inter-Agency Working Group on the Food Security Pillar of the G20 Multi-Year Action Plan on Development, 'Options for Promoting Responsible Investment in Agriculture', Report to the High-Level Working Group, September 2011.
6. Inter-Agency Working Group on the Principles for Responsible Agricultural Investment, Synthesis report on the field-testing of the Principles for Responsible Agricultural Investment, October 2012.

Intended users

While acknowledging that farmers are the largest investors in primary agriculture, the Guidance targets all enterprises operating along agricultural supply chains as detailed in Figure 1.1, including domestic and foreign, private and public, small, medium and large-scale enterprises, referred to as 'enterprises' throughout the Guidance.[10] It can also be used by governments, particularly NCPs, to better understand and promote existing standards in agricultural supply chains. Furthermore, it can help affected communities understand what they should expect from the above-mentioned actors and thus ensure that their rights are respected.

Process

The Guidance was developed by FAO and OECD through an inclusive consultation process led by a multi-stakeholder Advisory Group established in October 2013.[11] The Advisory Group comprises representatives from OECD and non-OECD members, institutional investors, agri-food companies, farmers' organisations, civil society organisations and international organisations. Its tasks are as follows:

- Provide substantive inputs for the development of the Guidance.
- Assist with the process of broadly consulting with other relevant stakeholders, including by providing inputs and participating in multi-stakeholder processes, in particular the meetings of the CFS-RAI Open-Ended Working Group.
- Provide substantive inputs on follow-up measures to effectively promote and implement the Guidance.

The FAO and OECD Secretariats coordinated the consultation process in co-operation with the Advisory Group and under the leadership of its Chair and Vice-Chairs. The OECD Working Party on Responsible Business Conduct, a subsidiary body of the Investment Committee, and the Working Party on Agricultural Policies and Markets, a subsidiary body of the OECD Committee for Agriculture, have been regularly consulted.

Key concepts

Agricultural supply chains

Agricultural supply chains refer to the system encompassing all the activities, organisations, actors, technology, information, resources and services involved in producing agri-food products for consumer markets. They cover agricultural upstream and downstream sectors from the supply of agricultural inputs (such as seeds, fertilisers, feeds, medicines, or equipment) to production, post-harvest handling, processing, transportation, marketing, distribution, and retailing. They also include support services such as extension services, research and development, and market information. As such, they consist of a wide range of enterprises, ranging from smallholders, farmers' organisations, co-operatives and start-up companies to MNEs through parent companies or their local affiliates, state-owned enterprises and funds, private financial actors and private foundations. Some actors have entered the sector in recent years.

The structure of supply chains and the enterprises involved at each stage vary significantly across products and geographies.[12] Mapping enterprises that operate along agricultural supply chains should thus be undertaken on a case-by-case basis, with a view to better understanding relationships and information and financial flows among these enterprises and to better designing audits. For the purpose of this Guidance, a simplified supply chain structure is proposed in Figure 1.1.

Enterprises are related through diverse relationships and arrangements. Downstream enterprises can engage in various types of relationships with on-farm enterprises to secure access to agricultural products. They can impose standards and specifications on producers with little involvement beyond a buying contract. But they can also be more actively involved, particularly through contract farming, in order to co-ordinate production and ensure quality and safety.[13] Financial enterprises may be involved in a more indirect way by providing capital to on-farm and downstream enterprises, through greenfield or brownfield investments, joint ventures or mergers and acquisitions. These categories are often difficult to delineate in practice. For instance, co-operatives often own or manage agricultural equipment as well as downstream assets (e.g. sugar mill) and could thus be considered not only as on-farm enterprises but also as downstream enterprises.

Figure 1.1. **Various stages of agricultural supply chains and enterprises involved**

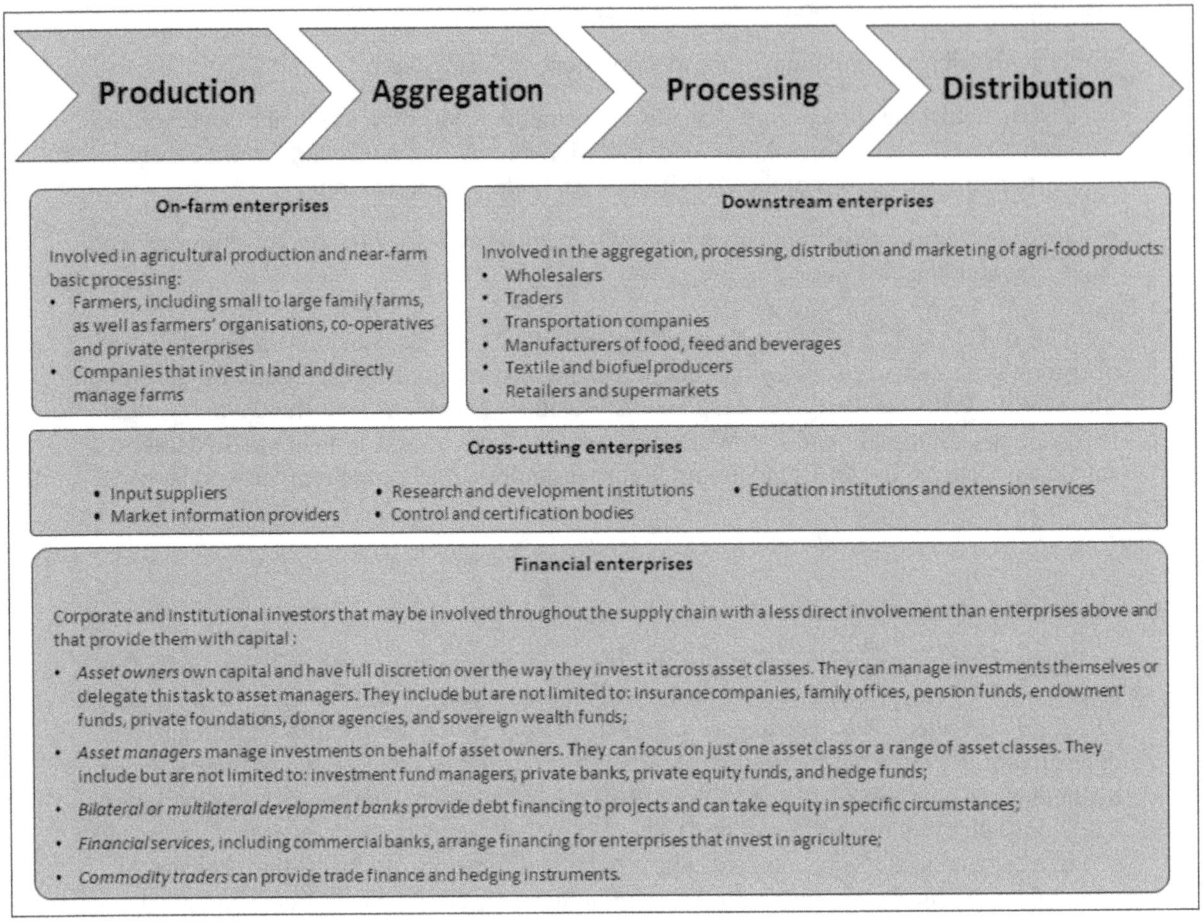

Production
Aggregation
Processing
Distribution
On-farm enterprises
Involved in agricultural production and near-farm basic processing:
• Farmers, including small to large family farms, as well as farmers' organisations, co-operatives and private enterprises
• Companies that invest in land and directly manage farms
Downstream enterprises
Involved in the aggregation, processing, distribution and marketing of agri-food products:
• Wholesalers
• Traders
• Transportation companies
• Manufacturers of food, feed and beverages
• Textile and biofuel producers
• Retailers and supermarkets
Cross-cutting enterprises
• Input suppliers
• Market information providers
• Research and development institutions
• Control and certification bodies
• Education institutions and extension services
Financial enterprises
Corporate and institutional investors that may be involved throughout the supply chain with a less direct involvement than enterprises above and that provide them with capital:
• Asset owners own capital and have full discretion over the way they invest it across asset classes. They can manage investments themselves or delegate this task to asset managers. They include but are not limited to: insurance companies, family offices, pension funds, endowment funds, private foundations, donor agencies, and sovereign wealth funds;
• Asset managers manage investments on behalf of asset owners. They can focus on just one asset class or a range of asset classes. They include but are not limited to: investment fund managers, private banks, private equity funds, and hedge funds;
• Bilateral or multilateral development banks provide debt financing to projects and can take equity in specific circumstances;
• Financial services, including commercial banks, arrange financing for enterprises that invest in agriculture;
• Commodity traders can provide trade finance and hedging instruments.

Note: This diagram is for reference only and does not aim at being comprehensive.

Figure 1.2. **Risks at various stages of agricultural supply chains**

STAGES
Production
Aggregation
Processing
Distribution
CROSS-CUTTING RISKS
Human rights
Labour rights
Health
Food security & nutrition
Access to natural resources
Environmental protection & sustainable use of resources
Gover-nance
Technology & innovation
MORE SPECIFIC RISKS
Animal welfare
Tenure rights

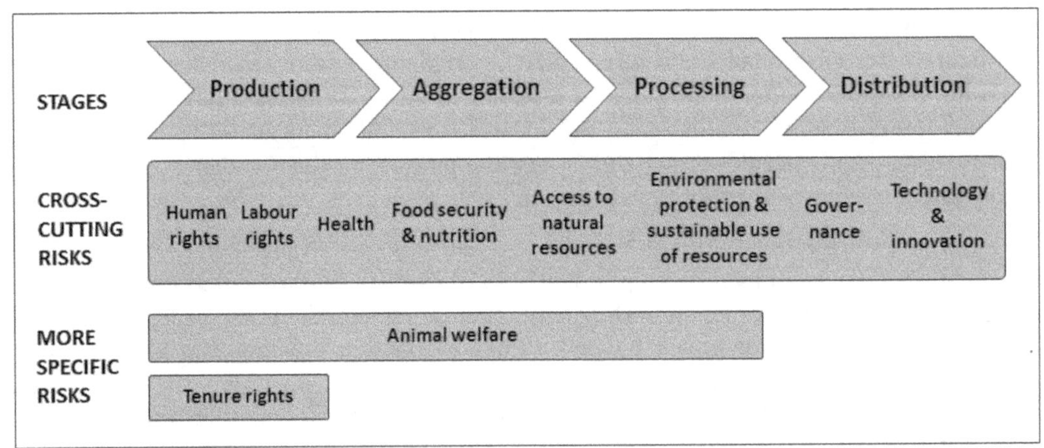

Depending on their situation along the supply chain, enterprises may focus on specific risks (Figure 1.2). For instance, on-farm enterprises face higher risks related to tenure rights. Thus they should focus particularly on undertaking good-faith, effective and meaningful consultations with tenure rights holders.

Due diligence

Due diligence is understood as the process through which enterprises can identify, assess, mitigate, prevent and account for how they address the actual and potential adverse impacts of their activities as an integral part of business decision-making and risk management systems.[14] It concerns adverse impacts caused or contributed to by enterprises as well as those adverse impacts that are directly linked to their operations, products or services through a business relationship (see Box 1.2 for further details).

Box 1.2. **Addressing adverse impacts**

Under the OECD Guidelines, enterprises should 'avoid causing or contributing to adverse impacts on matters covered by the Guidelines, through their own activities, and address such impacts when they occur.' They should also 'seek to prevent or mitigate an adverse impact where they have not contributed to that impact, when the impact is nevertheless directly linked to their operations, products or services by a business relationship. This is not intended to shift responsibility from the entity causing an adverse impact to the enterprise with which it has a business relationship.' For instance, a financial institution may contribute to an adverse impact caused by its investee company in which it has a majority or controlling holding.

An enterprise '*causes*' an adverse impact if there is causality between the operations, products or services of the enterprise and the adverse impact. Causation can occur through action as well as omissions, in other words, a failure to act. '*Contributing to*' an adverse impact should be interpreted as a substantial contribution, meaning an activity that causes, facilitates or incentivises another entity to cause an adverse impact. An enterprise can also contribute to an adverse impact if the combination of its activities and that of another entity result in an adverse impact. *'Directly linked'* is a broad concept and covers adverse impacts associated with business relationships. The term business relationship includes an enterprise's relationships with business partners, entities in the supply chain and any other non-state or state entities directly linked to its business operations, products or services. Entities with which an enterprise has a business relationship are referred to as *'business partners'* throughout the Guidance.

The OECD Guidelines underline that 'enterprises should 'encourage, where practicable, business partners, including suppliers and sub-contractors, to apply RBC principles compatible with the OECD Guidelines.' They further state that 'an enterprise, acting alone or in co-operation with other entities, as appropriate, should use its leverage[1] to influence the entity causing the adverse human rights impact to prevent or mitigate that impact.' Factors determining the appropriate action include 'the enterprise's leverage over the entity concerned, how crucial the relationship is to the enterprise, the severity of the impact, and whether terminating the relationship with the entity itself would have adverse human rights impacts.'

Thus, enterprises are expected to use their leverage over entities directly linked to their operations, products or services to support the implementation of this Guidance. For instance, if their business partners may be sourcing from or linked to any business partner violating legitimate tenure rights, they should work with them on corrective action and, to the extent possible, terminate the business relationship if no remedial action is taken.

1. Leverage is considered to exist where the enterprise has the ability to effect change in the wrongful practices of the entity that causes the harm.

Source: OECD Guidelines, II.A.11-13; II.A, para 14; and IV.43; OECD (2014).

Enterprises assess risks by identifying the factual circumstances of their activities and business relationships and evaluating those facts against applicable rights and duties under national and international law and standards, RBC recommendations of international organisations, government-backed tools, private voluntary initiatives and their own internal policies and systems. Due diligence can help enterprises and their business partners ensure they observe international and domestic law and RBC standards.

The nature and extent of due diligence will be affected by factors such as the size of the enterprise, the context and location of its operations, the nature of its products or services, and the severity of actual and potential adverse impacts.[15] While small and medium enterprises, particularly smallholders, may not have the capacity to carry out due diligence as recommended in this Guidance, they are encouraged to remain involved in the due diligence efforts of their customers in order to improve their capacity and be able to carry out proper due diligence in the future.

The OECD Guidelines recommend carrying out risk-based due diligence, meaning that the nature and extent of due diligence should correspond to the type and level of risk of adverse impacts.[16] The severity of actual and potential adverse impacts should determine the scale and complexity of the necessary due diligence. Higher risk areas should be subject to enhanced due diligence. When enterprises have large numbers of suppliers, they are encouraged to identify general areas where the risk of adverse impacts is most significant and, based on this risk assessment, prioritise suppliers for due diligence.[17] A risk-based approach should not prohibit enterprises from engaging in certain contexts or with certain business partners, but should assist them in effectively managing the risks of adverse impacts in high-risk contexts.

As detailed in Section 3, the various components of due diligence can be incorporated into the following five-step framework (Box 1.3).

Box 1.3. **Five-Step Framework for Due Diligence**

- Step 1: Establish strong enterprise management systems for responsible supply chains.
- Step 2: Identify, assess and prioritise risks in the supply chain.
- Step 3: Design and implement a strategy to respond to identified risks in the supply chain
- Step 4: Verify supply chain due diligence.
- Step 5: Report on supply chain due diligence.

Source: OECD (2013), *OECD Due Diligence Guidance for Responsible Supply Chains of Minerals from Conflict-Affected and High-Risk Areas: Second Edition*, OECD Publishing, Paris, http://dx.doi.org/10.1787/9789264185050-en.

As the same enterprise may cover various stages of the supply chain, ensuring good co-ordination across different departments of the enterprise can help implement due diligence. With due regard to competition and data privacy issues, enterprises can carry out due diligence by collaborating within the industry to ensure that the process is mutually reinforcing and reduce costs through:

- industry-wide co-operation, for instance through initiatives created and managed by an industry organisation to support and advance adherence to international standards[18]
- cost-sharing within industry for specific due diligence tasks
- co-ordination between industry members who share the same suppliers
- co-operation between different segments of the supply chain, such as upstream and downstream enterprises.

Partnerships with international and civil society organisations can also support due diligence. Industry-driven programmes are most credible when they involve not only business but also civil society organisations, trade unions and relevant experts and allow building consensus among them. However, enterprises retain individual responsibility for their due diligence.

Structure

The structure of the Guidance draws from the OECD Due Diligence Guidance for Responsible Supply Chains of Minerals from Conflict-Affected and High-Risk Areas,[19] which clarifies how the OECD Guidelines apply to a specific sector by proposing due diligence steps and risk mitigation measures. Following this introduction, the present Guidance includes:

- Section 1. A model enterprise policy which outlines the content of existing standards for responsible agricultural supply chains.
- Section 2. A framework for risk-based due diligence along agricultural supply chains.
- Annex A. A description of the risks and measures for risk mitigation along agricultural supply chains, drawing from existing standards.
- Annex B. Guidance for engaging with indigenous peoples.

2. Model enterprise policy for responsible agricultural supply chains

This model enterprise policy provides the major standards that enterprises should observe to build responsible agricultural supply chains. It does so by outlining parts of the content of the relevant international standards for responsible agricultural supply chains.[20] Some of these standards, e.g. for human and labour rights and food safety, have already been incorporated in the legislation of many countries.

This model enterprise policy can be adopted by enterprises as it is, or relevant parts can be incorporated into and tailored to their existing policies on corporate social responsibility, sustainability, risk management, or other equivalent alternatives. The use of "we" indicates the self-commitment of enterprises. When designing their policy, enterprises should also ensure that they comply with all applicable national laws and consider any other relevant international standards. Adopting a policy for responsible agricultural supply chains is the first step of the risk-based due-diligence framework outlined in Section 3 that describes how such a policy can be implemented.

Recognising the risks of significant adverse impacts arising along agricultural supply chains, and recognising our responsibility to respect human rights and our capacity to contribute to sustainable development, and in particular poverty reduction, food security and nutrition, and gender equality, we commit to adopt, implement, widely disseminate and incorporate in contracts and agreements with business partners the following policy for responsible agricultural supply chains. We will encourage, where practicable, our business partners to apply this policy and, if they cause or contribute to adverse impacts, we will use our leverage to prevent or mitigate these impacts.

1. Cross-cutting RBC standards

Impact assessment

We will continuously assess and address in decision-making the actual and potential impacts of our operations, processes, goods and services over their full life-cycle with a view to avoiding or, when unavoidable, mitigating any adverse impacts. Impact assessments should involve a representative number of all relevant stakeholder groups.[21]

Disclosure

We will disclose timely and accurate information related to foreseeable risk factors and our response to particular environmental, social and human rights impacts to potentially affected communities, at all stages of the investment cycle.[22] We will also provide accurate, verifiable and clear information that is sufficient to enable consumers to make informed decisions.[23]

Consultations

We will hold good-faith, effective and meaningful consultations with communities through their own representative institutions before initiating any operations that may affect them and we will continue to hold consultations with them during and at the end of operations. We will bear in mind the different risks that may be faced by women and men.[24]

We will hold effective and meaningful consultations with indigenous peoples through their own representative institutions in order to obtain their free, prior and informed consent[25] consistent with achieving the ends of the United Nations Declaration of Rights of Indigenous Peoples and with due regard for particular positions and understanding of individual states.[26]

Benefit sharing

We will ensure that our operations contribute to sustainable and inclusive rural development,[27] including, as appropriate, through promoting fair and equitable sharing of monetary and non-monetary benefits with affected communities on mutually agreed terms, in accordance with international treaties, where applicable for parties to such treaties, e.g. when using genetic resources for food and agriculture.[28]

Grievance mechanisms

We will provide for legitimate, accessible, predictable, equitable and transparent operational-level grievance mechanisms in consultation with potential users. We will also co-operate in other non-judicial grievance mechanisms. Such grievance mechanisms can enable remediation when our operations have caused or contributed to adverse impacts due to non-adherence to RBC standards.[29]

Gender

We will help eliminate discrimination against women, enhance their meaningful participation in decision-making and leadership roles, ensure their professional development and advancement, and facilitate their equal access and control over natural resources, inputs, productive tools, advisory and financial services, training, markets and information.[30]

2. Human rights

Within the framework of internationally recognised human rights,[31] the international human rights obligations of the countries in which we operate as well as relevant domestic laws and regulations, we will:

- Respect human rights,[32] which means avoid infringing on the human rights of others and address adverse human rights impacts with which we are involved.
- Within the context of our own activities, avoid causing or contributing to adverse human rights impacts and address such impacts when they occur.[33]
- Seek ways to prevent or mitigate adverse human rights impacts that are directly linked to our operations, products or services by a business relationship, even if we did not contribute to those impacts.[34]

- Carry out human rights due diligence as appropriate to the size, nature and context of our operations and the severity of the risks of adverse human rights impacts.[35]
- Provide for, or co-operate through legitimate processes in, the remediation of adverse impacts on human rights when we identify that we have caused or contributed to these impacts.[36]
- Within the context of our own activities, ensure that all persons' human rights are respected, without distinction of any kind, such as race, colour, sex, language, religion, political or other opinion, national or social origin, property, birth or other status.[37]

3. Labour rights

We will respect international core labour standards in our operations, namely the freedom of association and the right to collective bargaining, including for migrant workers, the elimination of all forms of forced or compulsory labour, the effective abolition of child labour and the elimination of discrimination in respect of employment and occupation.[38]

In our operations, we will also:

- Ensure occupational health and safety.
- Ensure decent wages, benefits and working conditions, that are at least adequate to satisfy the basic needs of workers and their families, and strive to improve working conditions.[39]
- Promote the security of employment and co-operate in government schemes to provide some form of income protection to workers whose employment has been terminated.[40]
- Seek to prevent abuses of migrant workers.[41]
- Adopt approaches, measures, and processes to enhance women's meaningful participation in decision-making and leadership roles.[42]

We will contribute to the realisation of the right to work,[43] by:

- striving to increase employment opportunities, both directly and indirectly[44]
- ensuring that relevant training is provided for all levels of employees, to meet the needs of the enterprise and the development policies of the host country, including by increasing the productivity of the youth and/or their access to decent employment and entrepreneurship opportunities[45]
- ensuring maternity protection at work.[46]

4. Health and safety

We will promote public health[47] by:

- adopting appropriate practices to prevent threats to human life, health, and welfare in our operations, as well as threats deriving from the consumption, use or disposal of our goods and services, including by adhering to good practices in food safety[48]
- contributing to the protection of the health and safety of affected communities during the life-cycle of our operations.[49]

5. Food security and nutrition

We will strive to ensure that our operations contribute to food security and nutrition. We will give attention to enhancing the availability, accessibility, stability and utilisation of safe, nutritious and diverse foods.[50]

6. Tenure rights over and access to natural resources

We will respect legitimate tenure right holders[51] and their rights over natural resources, including public, private, communal, collective, indigenous and customary rights, potentially affected by our activities. Natural resources include land, fisheries, forests, and water.

To the greatest extent possible, we will commit to transparency and information disclosure on our land-based investments, including transparency of lease/concession contract terms, with due regard to privacy restrictions.[52]

We will give preference to feasible alternative project designs to avoid or, when avoidance is not possible, minimise the physical and/or economic displacement of legitimate tenure right holders, while balancing environmental, social, and financial costs and benefits, paying particular attention to adverse impacts on the poor and vulnerable.

We are aware that, subject to their national law and legislation and in accordance with national context, states should expropriate only where the rights at issue are required for a public purpose and should ensure a prompt, adequate and effective compensation.[53]

When holders of legitimate tenure rights are negatively affected, we will seek to ensure that they receive a prompt, adequate and effective compensation of their tenure rights being negatively impacted by our operations.[54]

7. Animal welfare

We will support animal welfare in our operations,[55] including by:

- striving to ensure that the 'five freedoms' for animal welfare are implemented, i.e. freedom from hunger, thirst and malnutrition, physical and thermal discomfort, pain, injury and disease, fear and distress, and freedom to express normal patterns of behaviour[56]
- ensuring high standards of management and stockmanship for animal production, that are appropriate to the scale of our operations, in accordance with or exceeding OIE's principles.[57]

8. Environmental protection and sustainable use of natural resources

We will establish and maintain, in co-ordination with responsible government agencies and third parties as appropriate, an environmental and social management system appropriate to the nature and scale of our operations and commensurate with the level of potential environmental and social risks and impacts.[58]

We will continuously improve our environmental performance by:

- preventing, minimising and remedying pollution and negative impacts on air, land, soil, water, forests and biodiversity, and reducing greenhouse gas emissions

- avoiding or reducing the generation of hazardous and non-hazardous waste, substituting or reducing the use of toxic substances,[59] and enhancing the productive use or ensuring a safe disposal of waste
- ensuring the sustainable use of natural resources and increasing the efficiency of resource use and energy[60]
- reducing food loss and waste and promoting recycling
- promoting good agricultural practices, including to maintain or improve soil fertility and avoid soil erosion
- supporting and conserving biodiversity, genetic resources and ecosystem services; respecting protected areas,[61] high conservation value areas and endangered species; and controlling and minimising the spread of invasive non-native species
- increasing the resilience of agriculture and food systems, the supporting habitats and related livelihoods to the effects of climate change through adaptation measures.[62]

9. Governance

We will prevent and abstain from any form of corruption and fraudulent practices.[63]

We will comply with both the letter and spirit of the tax laws and regulations of the countries in which we operate.[64]

We will refrain from entering into or carrying out anti-competitive agreements among competitors and will co-operate with investigating competition authorities.[65]

To the extent to which they apply to enterprises, we will act consistently with the Principles contained in the OECD Recommendation of the Council on Principles of Corporate Governance.[66]

10. Technology and innovation

We will contribute to the development and diffusion of appropriate technologies, particularly environmentally-friendly technologies and those that generate direct and indirect employment.[67]

3. Five-step framework for risk-based due diligence along agricultural supply chains

Enterprises should implement the following five-step framework to undertake risk-based due diligence along agricultural supply chains: (i) establish strong enterprise management systems for responsible agricultural supply chains; (ii) identify, assess and prioritise risks in the supply chain; (iii) design and implement a strategy to respond to identified risks; (iv) verify supply chain due diligence; and (v) report on supply chain due diligence. The first step includes the adoption of an enterprise policy for RBC that can draw from the model enterprise policy in Section 2 of the Guidance. While all enterprises should conduct due diligence, the implementation of this five-step framework should be tailored to their position and the type of involvement in the supply chain, the context and location of their operations, as well as their size and capacities. To the extent possible, this section differentiates the responsibilities of various types of enterprises (on-farm, downstream and financial enterprises) at each step.

Step 1. Establish strong enterprise management systems for responsible agricultural supply chains

1.1 Adopt, or integrate into existing processes, an enterprise policy for RBC along the supply chain (hereafter 'enterprise policy for RBC')

This policy should incorporate the standards against which due diligence is to be conducted, drawing from international standards and the model enterprise policy above. It can consist of one single policy or several stand-alone policies (e.g. enterprise policy on human rights) and can include the commitment to adhere to existing industry-specific standards, such as certification schemes.[68] If long-standing policies are in place, a gap analysis can determine gaps in comparison with the model enterprise policy in Section 2 and existing policies can be updated accordingly.

The enterprise policy for RBC should:

- be approved at the most senior level of the enterprise. Senior level responsibility should be assigned for its implementation.
- be informed by relevant internal and external expertise, and as appropriate, stakeholder consultations
- stipulate the enterprise's expectations in terms of RBC of employees, business partners and other parties directly linked to its operations, products or services
- be publicly available and communicated to all employees, business partners and other relevant parties

- be reflected in operational policies and procedures necessary to embed it throughout the enterprise[69]
- be reviewed and adapted on a regular basis in light of the increasing knowledge about risks in the supply chain and international standards.

While some risks of adverse impacts arise at specific stages of the supply chain, such as the production and processing stages for land tenure and animal welfare, the enterprise policy for RBC should cover the risks arising throughout the entire supply chain.

1.2. Structure internal management to support supply chain due diligence

Senior management should be visibly and actively involved in implementing and ensuring compliance with the enterprise policy for RBC. Employees and business partners should be trained and provided incentives to comply with it. An individual with relevant technical and cultural skills should be designated to be responsible for due diligence with the necessary support team. Adequate financial resources should be made available. An internal reporting structure should be set, maintained and communicated within the enterprise at key junctures. RBC practices should be consistent throughout the operations of the enterprise. These measures should be tailored to the purpose, activity, products and size of the enterprise, taking into consideration its financial capacities.

1.3. Establish a system of controls and transparency along the supply chain

Monitoring the implementation of the enterprise policy for RBC is critical to the credibility and effectiveness of the policy and to good relationships with stakeholders, including governments. It entails:

- Creating internal verification procedures to undertake regular independent and transparent reviews of compliance with the policy. Such procedure can consist of a traceability system[70] which implies: creating internal documentation of due diligence processes, findings and resulting decisions; maintaining internal inventory and transaction documentation that can be used retrospectively to identify actors in the supply chain; making and receiving payments through official banking and ensuring that all unavoidable cash purchases are supported by verifiable documentation; and maintaining the information collected for a period of several years. Upstream enterprises should establish mass balance or physical segregation traceability,[71] for instance through a chain of custody, while downstream enterprises should identify their upstream suppliers and the sourcing countries of their upstream sub-suppliers. Due diligence information passed on from upstream to downstream enterprises can increase transparency and facilitate traceability.
- Establishing permanent business relations as the best means for a continual flow of information. Channels for communicating with various stakeholders can warn of possible deviations from the policy and relevant standards. The execution and follow-up of periodic audits and of environmental, social and human rights impact assessments (ESHRIAs)[72] can also help assess compliance but should not substitute for such information flows.

1.4. Strengthen engagement with business partners

A policy for RBC, drawing from the enterprise policy for RBC, should be incorporated into contracts and agreements with business partners. It should be tailored to their capacities. Long-term relationships with business partners can increase leverage to encourage the adoption of such policy and improve transparency. Implementation plans developed in co-ordination with business partners and involving local and central governments, international organisations, and civil society, can also improve compliance, in particular by offering capacity-building trainings. For instance, enterprises can build the capacities of small-scale farmers that might have difficulties meeting stringent requirements that can be costly.

1.5. Establish an operational-level grievance mechanism in consultation and collaboration with relevant stakeholders

A grievance mechanism[73] can help alert enterprises to deviations from relevant standards and help them identify risks, including by allowing for improved communication with relevant stakeholders. It can be established at the level of a project, an enterprise or an industry. It should be used as an early-warning risk-awareness system and as a mechanism to prevent conflicts and provide redress. For instance, grievance mechanisms established by existing industrial relations systems and collective bargaining agreements can constitute effective and credible mechanisms to respect labour rights.

Grievance mechanisms should be easily accessible by workers and all those actually or potentially affected by the adverse impacts deriving from the enterprise's failure to uphold RBC standards. Enterprises should publicise their existence and modalities of access, actively encourage their use, guarantee that their users remain anonymous and free from reprisal, and regularly verify their effectiveness. They should keep a public registry of complaints received, and lessons learnt through grievance mechanisms should be incorporated in the enterprise policy for RBC, relations with business partners and monitoring systems.

Grievance mechanisms should complement judicial and other non-judicial mechanisms, such as NCPs, with which enterprises should also engage.

Step 2. Identify, assess and prioritise risks in the supply chain

2.1. Map the supply chain

This requires identifying the various actors involved, including, when relevant, the names of immediate suppliers and business partners and the sites of operations. For instance, the following details can be requested from on-farm enterprises: name of the producer unit; address and site identification; contact details of the site manager; category, quantity, dates and methods of production; number of workers by gender; list of risk management practices; transportation routes; and risk assessments that have been undertaken.

Enterprises, particularly financial enterprises and consumer-facing enterprises that are several tiers removed from agricultural production, may not be able to map all their suppliers and business partners initially. However, they should systematically work towards a complete picture of their business relationships. The extent of information collected on business partners depends on the severity of risks and on how closely linked to the identified risks they are.

2.2. Assess the risks of adverse environmental, social and human rights impacts[74] of the operations, processes, goods and services of the enterprise and its business partners over their full life cycle

Such assessments should identify the full extent of actual and potential adverse impacts in the supply chain either caused or contributed to by the enterprise or directly linked to its operations, products or services by a business relationship. They should cover environmental, social and human rights impacts. They may be required and regulated by domestic laws. Their scope and frequency should reflect the severity of the risks and the performance of business partners in managing them. They can be used for disclosure purposes but also in a more practical and forward-looking way to address specific risks, strengthen supplier dialogue, and improve supplier performance.

Drawing from existing standards, Annex A (Section 1.3) provides details on what stages and impacts these assessments should include. In addition, these assessments should identify:[75]

- relevant rights holders and stakeholders, particularly women, likely to be affected by the operations on an ongoing basis[76]
- any business partner that risks not undertaking proper due diligence
- any 'red flags' as described in Box 3.1. In such situations, enhanced due diligence may be needed, which could include on-the-ground verification of qualitative circumstances for red flag locations, products, or business partners
- any reasonable inconsistency between the factual circumstances of the operations and the enterprise policy for RBC.

Several **types of assessments** can help identify red flags. Context risk assessments categorise sourcing regions and countries as low, medium or high risk for specific risk areas by assessing the regulatory framework, political context, civil liberties and socio-economic environment. Site-level risk assessments aim to understand the factual circumstances of the operations of business partners in order to assess the scope, severity and likelihood of risks at the site level. They should form the basis of the pre-qualification process of new business partners. A standard risk assessment should be applied to business partners operating in low risk contexts. An enhanced risk assessment should be applied to all business partners operating in medium and high risk contexts. Assessments can include undertaking stakeholder consultations, monitoring by a third party, such as civil society organisations, and organising visits of the farms and/or processing facilities.

Risk assessment should be an **ongoing process** in order to maintain a true picture of the risks over time, taking into account changing circumstances. The following situations should trigger new risk assessments: sourcing from a new market; changes in the operating environment of a business partner (e.g. change in government); supplier begins sourcing from medium or high risk areas; start of a new business relationship; change in ownership of a business partner; development of a new product; or change in business model.

Box 3.1. **Examples of situations that warrant enhanced due diligence: Red flags**

- **Red flag locations - Operations are planned in or agricultural products originate from areas:**
  - affected by conflicts or considered as high-risk areas[1]
  - considered as weak governance areas[2]
  - where national or local governments do not observe internationally agreed RBC standards or do not provide support to the enterprise to ensure the observance of these standards, such as by proposing agricultural land on which local communities have legitimate tenure rights and have not been consulted, or which is located in protected areas
  - where violations of human rights or labour rights have been reported
  - where tenure rights are weakly defined or contested
  - where communities face food insecurity or water shortages
  - affected by environmental degradation or defined as protected areas.
- **Red flag products**
  - The production of the agricultural commodity is known to have adverse environmental, social or human rights impacts in certain contexts.
  - The agri-food product does not conform to health and food safety standards.
- **Red flag business partners**
  - Business partners are known not to have observed the standards contained in this Guidance.
  - They are known to have sourced agricultural products from a red flag location in the last twelve months.
  - They have shareholder or other interests in enterprises that do not observe the standards contained in this Guidance or that supply agricultural products from or operate in a red flag location.

1. Conflict-affected and high-risk areas are identified by the presence of armed conflict, widespread violence or other risks of harm to people. Armed conflict may take a variety of forms, such as a conflict of international or non-international character, which may involve two or more states, or may consist of wars of liberation, insurgencies, or civil wars, etc. High-risk areas may include areas of political instability or repression, institutional weakness, insecurity, collapse of civil infrastructure and widespread violence. Such areas are often characterised by widespread human rights abuses and violations of national or international law (OECD, 2013).
2. This may include areas showing poor performance as per the World Bank Worldwide Governance Indicators or Transparency International Corruption Perception Index. It could also include countries that have not committed to or started to implement the provisions of the United Nations Convention Against Corruption.

Risk assessments depend on the **type of enterprise:**

- On-farm enterprises may establish on-the-ground assessment teams for generating and sharing verifiable, reliable and up-to-date information on the qualitative circumstances of agricultural production. These enterprises would need to ensure that they respect legitimate land tenure right holders, including by holding good-faith, effective and meaningful consultations with local communities. If involved in livestock production, they should support animal welfare in their operations. They should provide the results of their risk assessments to downstream enterprises.

- Downstream enterprises should not only identify risks in their own operations but also, to the best of their efforts, assess the risks faced by their suppliers. They can assess the latter by assessing the due diligence carried out by their suppliers or by directly assessing the operations of their suppliers, for instance by conducting farm visits. Participating in industry-wide schemes that assess the compliance of business partners with RBC standards and provide relevant information can support these assessments.

- Financial enterprises may have hundreds to thousands of clients. It may not always be feasible to conduct risk assessments for each of them. Under the OECD Guidelines, all enterprises are expected to identify general areas where the risk of adverse impacts is most significant and to prioritise due diligence accordingly. The appropriate scope of due diligence responsibilities of a financial institution depends on the nature of its operations, products and services.[77]

Step 3. Design and implement a strategy to respond to identified risks

3.1. Report the findings of the risk assessment to the designated senior management

3.2. Adopt a risk management plan

This plan can include the risk mitigation and prevention measures suggested in Annex A. It can propose various scenarios depending on how closely the enterprise is linked to adverse impacts (see Box 1.2 for further details):

- If the enterprise is causing adverse impacts, it should provide remedy[78] for actual adverse impacts and prevent potential adverse impacts. This may entail suspending operations temporarily while undertaking measurable efforts to prevent any future adverse impacts, or suspending operations permanently if these impacts cannot be mitigated.

- If the enterprise is contributing to adverse impacts, it should cease its contribution to adverse impacts and use its leverage to mitigate any remaining adverse impacts. This may entail suspending operations temporarily. The enterprise should also take preventive measures to ensure that these adverse impacts will not re-occur.

- If the enterprise has not contributed to the adverse impact, when the impact is nevertheless directly linked to its operations, products or services by a business relationship, it should use its leverage to mitigate or prevent the adverse impact. This may lead to disengaging with a business partner after failed attempts at mitigating risks or when risk mitigation is deemed as not feasible or unacceptable. Factors that are relevant to determining the appropriate response include: the severity and probability of the adverse impact, the enterprise's ability to influence and/or build leverage over the business partner or other relevant actors (e.g. government), and how crucial the business partner is to the enterprise.

All types of enterprises may be directly causing, contributing to or directly linked to adverse impacts. The following examples illustrate what this can entail in practice:

- *Causing:* The three types of enterprises, on-farm, downstream and financial enterprises, can directly cause adverse impacts. However, some adverse impacts may be directly caused only by on-farm, and to a lesser extent, downstream enterprises, such as impacts on land tenure rights and animal welfare. If, in a risk assessment, an on-farm enterprise is found infringing the land rights of legitimate rights holders, it should provide remedy for such impacts, e.g. return the land to the legitimate rights holders or ensure that they receive a fair and prompt compensation.
- *Contributing to:* If a large food retailer requires tight delivery schedules of seasonal and fresh agricultural products, such as strawberries, it may lead its suppliers to suddenly increase their workforce to meet the demand, and thus generate abuses of temporary migrant workers. The food retailer should thus cease its contribution to this adverse impact by, for instance, easing the pressure on its supplier or increasing purchasing prices to take into account the cash flow constraints of its suppliers.
- *Directly linked to:* A pension fund can invest in an investment fund that in turn invests in a farm that relies on child labour for some of the most labour intensive tasks, such as vanilla harvesting. The pension fund is thus directly linked to adverse human rights impacts. It should use its leverage to prevent or mitigate the adverse impact, for instance by expressing its intention to divest from the investment fund if child labour is not addressed at the farm level.

3.3. Implement the risk management plan, monitor and track performance of risk mitigation efforts and report back to the designated senior management

This entails consulting with affected stakeholders, including workers and their representatives, and business partners, to clarify concerns and agree on the strategy for mitigating risks.

Step 4. Verify supply chain due diligence

Enterprises should take steps to verify that their due diligence practices are effective, i.e. that risks have been adequately identified and mitigated or prevented. Two scenarios arise:

1. If the risk has been mitigated or prevented, the enterprise should conduct on-going due diligence proportionate to the risk.
2. If the risk has not been mitigated or prevented, the verification process should identify why this is the case, such as the lack of effective risk mitigation strategy, or inadequate timing, resources or lack of will to mitigate risks. A new risk assessment should be undertaken.

The verification process should:

- Ensure that the voice of women is adequately represented.

- Be proportionate to the risk.
- Generate recommendations to improve due diligence practices.
- Take into account the capacities of various enterprises as such processes can be costly. Due diligence may be assessed through affordable mechanisms for small enterprises, such as locally-driven social compliance initiatives.[79]

The verification process may include audits, on-site investigations, and consultations with government authorities, civil society, members of the affected community, and workers' organisations at local, national and international level. The independence and quality of audits are critical to their effectiveness.[80] Auditors should be independent, competent and accountable. Enterprises may consider incorporating audits into an independent institutionalised mechanism responsible for accrediting auditors, verifying audits, publishing audit reports, implementing modules to build capabilities of suppliers to conduct due diligence, and helping follow up on grievances of interested parties.

Complementary and mutually-reinforcing verification processes based on common standards, undertaken at appropriate points in the supply chain, can help avoid assessment fatigue and increase efficiency.[81] For instance, auditors may recognise the conclusions of audits carried out by other independent third parties. Enterprises may wish to focus on 'choke points', i.e. points at which a narrow set of stakeholders is operating in the supply chain - as opposed to every enterprise in the supply chain being assessed. They can identify choke points by taking into consideration:

i) key points of material transformation in the supply chain, such as processing or packaging

ii) number of actors at a given point in the supply chain: audits could focus on points in the supply chain where relatively few actors are active or where most agri-food products are aggregated

iii) greatest points of leverage of downstream enterprises

iv) points where schemes and audit programmes already exist to leverage these systems and avoid duplication.

For instance, a possible choke point for the coffee supply chain in Ethiopia could be the Ethiopian Commodity Exchange where a limited number of traders sell the coffee produced by numerous small producers (case ii. above). In more fragmented coffee supply chains, choke points could be processing factories, wholesalers or exporters. The focus on these choke points should not substitute a thorough due diligence carried out throughout the supply chain.

Step 5. Report on supply chain due diligence

Enterprises should publicly report on their supply chain due diligence policies and practices, with due regard taken of business confidentiality and other competitive concerns. They should provide affected stakeholders and business partners with clear, accurate and timely information on actual and potential adverse impacts identified through ongoing impact assessments and on the steps and measures taken to mitigate or prevent them. Reports may also include information on the enterprise management systems and the verification reports of due diligence practices. Once released, they should be accessible to all relevant stakeholders.

Beyond public and formal reporting, communication can take a variety of forms, including in-person meetings, online dialogues, and consultation with affected stakeholders. Communication needs to be appropriate to the impacts and audience in terms of its form, frequency, accessibility, and the adequacy of information provided.

Notes

1. While the Constitution of the Food and Agriculture Organization of the United Nations (FAO) includes fisheries and forestry in the definition of agriculture, the present Guidance focuses mostly on crops and livestock.

2. Responsible Business Conduct (RBC) means that businesses should: a) make a positive contribution to economic, environmental and social progress with a view to achieving sustainable development and b) avoid and address adverse impacts of their own activities and prevent or mitigate adverse impacts directly linked to their operations, products or services by a business relationship.

3 Throughout this Guidance, standards refer to recommendations contained in various types of instruments, including conventions, declarations, principles and guidelines.

4. As underlined in the 2015 report of the World Economic Forum *'Beyond supply chains - Empowering responsible value chains'*, observing RBC standards can benefit enterprises as changing market dynamics increase the importance of sustainability efforts. Customers are becoming more sensitive to sustainability. Younger consumers in particular demand sustainable products and practices and will pay more to get them. Increasingly scarce natural resources and rising commodity prices make resource efficiency and waste reduction crucial variables for enterprises to remain profitable. The regulatory environment and non-governmental organisations are pushing for more transparency, which drives non-compliance costs and can create a backlash from the marketplace.

5. See the definition of due diligence further below for a definition of 'business relationship'.

6. See the section 'intended users' for a more detailed description.

7. Additional resources are available at: *http://mneguidelines.oecd.org/rbc-agriculture-supply-chains.htm and www.fao.org/economic/est/issues/investment/en*.

8. See the sub-section 'process' for further details on the composition and the role of the Advisory Group in developing this Guidance.

9. Additional information is available at: *http://mneguidelines.oecd.org/rbc-agriculture-supply-chains.htm*.

10. While the OECD Guidelines do not provide a precise definition of multinational enterprises (MNEs), they indicate that MNEs usually comprise companies or other entities established in more than one country (OECD Guidelines, I.4). The CFS-RAI Principles target 'business enterprises, including farmers' (paras. 50-52).

11. The terms of reference of the Multi-Stakeholder Advisory Group defining its objectives, tasks and organisational structure were endorsed by the OECD Working Party on Responsible Business Conduct in June 2013 and by the OECD Working Party on Agricultural Policies and Markets in July 2013.

12. For specific examples, see: Botswana agrifood value chain project: Beef value chain study by the FAO in 2013; A farm gate-to-consumer value chain analysis of Kenya's maize marketing system by Michigan State University in 2011; Value chain analysis of the cashew sector in Ghana by GIZ in 2010; or Rwanda's essential oils value chains: A diagnostic by UNIDO in 2012.

13. Contract farming involves production carried out on the basis of an agreement between the buyer and the producer. It covers a wide range of contracts and differs by type of contractor, type of product, intensity of coordination between farmers and investors, and the number of stakeholders involved. For further information, see *www.fao.org/ag/ags/contract-farming/faq/en/#c100440*.

14. For further details, see the OECD Due Diligence for Responsible Supply Chains of Minerals from Conflict-Affected and High-Risk Areas, 2011.

15. Drawing from OECD Guidelines, II.15.

16. OECD Guidelines, II.A.10.

17. OECD Guidelines, II.16.

18. Such programmes include among others: Principles and criteria for sustainable palm oil production which certifies palm oil producers, processors or traders, as well as manufacturers, retailers, banks and investors involved in palm oil supply chains; standards of the roundtable on sustainable biofuels which certifies biofuel operators; Principles and criteria for responsible soy production certifying soy growers and soy growers' groups; Better Sugar Cane Initiative (Bonsucro) Standards for sugarcane producers; and Principles for Responsible Investment in Farmland for institutional asset owners and managers. Monitoring platforms such as Sedex can also help monitor suppliers' performance.

19. The OECD Recommendation on the Due Diligence Guidance for Responsible Supply Chains of Minerals from Conflict-Affected and High-Risk Areas was adopted by Council at Ministerial level on 25 May 2011 and subsequently amended on 17 July 2012 to include a reference to the Supplement on Gold.

20. The model enterprise policy does not aim to substitute existing standards. Enterprises should refer directly to each of these standards before making any claims regarding their observance. References to the standards cited throughout the document are indicated after the last element mentioned and not after each of the elements cited. They aim to help enterprises refer to the initial text of the standards considered in this Guidance for further details on the content of such standards.

21. OECD Guidelines, II.10 and VI.3; CFS-RAI Principle 10; VGGT 12.10; UN Guiding Principles, para. 17; CBD, Article 14; Akwé: Kon Guidelines; IFC Performance Standard 1, paras 5 and 8-10.

22. OECD Guidelines, III.1-3, VI.2.a & VIII.2; CFS-RAI Principles 9.ii and 10; UN Guiding Principles, para. 21; IFC Performance Standard 1, para. 29; Aarhus Convention, Article 5. See Annex A, 1.1 and 1.3 below. Specific guidance on material information to be shared with affected stakeholders can be found in the OECD Due Diligence Guidance for Meaningful Stakeholder Engagement in the Extractive Sector.

23. OECD Guidelines, VIII.2.

24. OECD Guidelines, II.14 & VI.2.b; CFS-RAI Principle 9.iii-iv; VGGT, 9.9 and 12.11; UN Guiding Principle, para. 18; PRAI Principles 1 and 4; Akwé: Kon Guidelines, 11, 13-17 and 57; IFC Performance Standard 1, para. 26-27 and 30-33. See also ILO Convention No. 169 on Indigenous and Tribal Peoples, 1989. See Annex A, 1.2 below. Further guidance on stakeholder engagement can be found in the OECD Due Diligence Guidance for Meaningful Stakeholder Engagement in the Extractive Sector.

25. See Annex B for further guidance on engagement with indigenous peoples and free, prior and informed consent (FPIC).

26. As underlined in the introduction, as a joint endeavour of OECD and FAO, this Guidance considers several standards other than the OECD Guidelines, particularly the CFS-RAI Principles, which include references to FPIC not found in the OECD Guidelines. This paragraph quotes CFS-RAI Principle 9.iv. See also IFC Performance Standard 7, paras. 12-17; Akwé: Kon Guidelines, 29 and 60; VGGT, 3B.6, 9.9 and 12.7; UN Declaration on the Rights of Indigenous Peoples, Articles 10, 11 and 32; and ILO Convention No. 169 on Indigenous and Tribal Peoples, Article 16.

27. OECD Guidelines, II.A.1; CFS-RAI Principle 2.iv, v and vii; VGGT, 12.4; Akwé: Kon Guidelines, 40.

28. CFS-RAI Principles 2.iv-vii and 7.i & iii; VGGT, 12.6; PRAI Principles 5-6; Akwé: Kon Guidelines, 46; IFC Performance Standard 7, paras 14 and 17-20 and Standard 8, para 16. See also CBD Article 8(j), Nagoya Protocol Articles 5-7, ITPGR, Article 9.2. Benefits can be monetary and non-monetary: see Annex to the Nagoya Protocol. See also Annex A, 1.4 for further details.

29. OECD Guidelines, IV, para 46 and VIII.3; CFS-RAI Principle 9.v; VGGT, 3.2, 12.14, 25.1 & 25.3; UN Guiding Principle 31; PRAI Principle 1; Akwé: Kon Guidelines, 63; ILO MNE Declaration, 58-59; IFC Performance Standard 1, para 35, and IFC Performance Standard 5, para 11. See also Annex A, 1.5. The OECD Due Diligence Guidance for Meaningful Stakeholder Engagement in the Extractive Sector provides further guidance on grievance mechanisms.

30. CFS-RAI Principle 3; Convention on the Elimination of All Forms of Discrimination Against Women (CEDAW).

31. For more details on internationally recognised human rights, you can refer to OECD Guidelines, VI. 39.

32. OECD Guidelines, II.A.2 and IV; CFS-RAI Principles 1, 9.iv and 10 and Paras 3, 19.i, 47.v, 50 and 51; UN Guiding Principles, para. 11. See Annex A, 2.

33. OECD Guidelines, IV.1 and 2.

34. OECD Guidelines, IV.3; VGGT, 3.2; PRAI Principle 1; Akwe: Kon Guidelines, 57; UN Global Compact, Principles 1-2.

35. OECD Guidelines, IV.5; UN Guiding Principle 17.

36. OECD Guidelines, IV.6; UN Guiding Principle 22.

37. Universal Declaration of Human Rights, Article 2; CFS-RAI Principles 3.ii. As highlighted in Annex A, the OECD Guidelines (V.1.e) state that enterprises should 'be guided throughout their operations by the principle of equality of opportunity and treatment in employment and not discriminate against their workers with respect to employment or occupation on such grounds as race, colour, sex, religion, political

opinion, national extraction or social origin, or other status'. Commentary 54 specifies that the term "other status" for the purposes of the Guidelines refers to trade union activity and personal characteristics such as age, disability, pregnancy, marital status, sexual orientation, or HIV status.

38. OECD Guidelines, V.1-3; CFS-RAI Principle 2.i-ii; ILO MNE Declaration, para 8; UN Guiding Principles, 12; IFC Performance Standard 2; Children's Rights and Business Principle 2. All ILO members have to respect these core labour standards that constitute the four fundamental principles of the ILO Declaration on Fundamental Principles and Rights at Work, regardless of which ILO convention they have ratified.

39. OECD Guidelines, V.4.b and V.4.c; CFS-RAI Principle 2.iii; ILO MNE Declaration 37-40; IFC Performance Standard 2, paras 10, 23, 25, 28-29; Children's Rights and Business Principles 3 and 4.

40. ILO MNE Declaration, 16 and 25-28. For further details, see Annex A, 3 on decent working conditions.

41. ILO Recommendation 198, Article 7.a; IFC Performance Standard 2, para 11.

42. CFS-RAI Principle 3.iv.

43. Universal Declaration of Human Rights, Article 23.

44. OECD Guidelines, II. A.4; ILO MNE Declaration, paras. 16 and 19; CFS-RAI Principle 2.iii.

45. CFS-RAI Principles 2,iii and 4.ii; ILO MNE Declaration 30-32.

46. ILO Maternity Protection Convention, 2000 (No. 183); Convention on the Elimination of All Forms of Discrimination Against Women, article 11 (2).

47. CFS-RAI Principle 8.iv.

48. OECD Guidelines, VIII.1, 6-7; CFS-RAI Principles 2.viii and 8.i, iii and iv; PRAI, 5.2.1.

49. Akwé Kon Guidelines, 50; IFC Performance Standard 4.

50. CFS-RAI Principle 1 and 8.i; VGGT 12.1, 12.4 and 12.12; PRAI Principle 2.2. See Annex A, 5. The four elements of food security, i.e. food availability, accessibility, stability and utilisation, are reflected in the World Food Summit Plan of Action of 1996 adopted by 112 Heads or Deputy Heads of State and Government who commit to *'implement policies aimed at eradicating poverty and inequality and improving physical and economic access by all, at all times, to sufficient, nutritionally adequate and safe food and its effective utilisation; and pursue participatory and sustainable food, agriculture, fisheries, forestry and rural development policies and practices in high and low potential areas, which are essential to adequate and reliable food supplies at the household, national, regional and global levels.'*

51. The VGGT 4.4 define legitimate tenure rights as follows: *'Consistent with the principles of consultation and participation of these Guidelines, States should define through widely publicized rules the categories of rights that are considered legitimate.'*

52. VGGT, 2.4, 3.2, 9.1, 11.4 and 12.3; CFS-RAI Principles 5 and 9.ii and Para 51; UN Principles for Responsible Contracts appended to the UN Guiding Principles and endorsed by the UN Human Rights Council, Principle 10.

53. VGGT, 9.1, 12.4, 16.1 and 16.3; IFC Performance Standard 5, paras. 2 and 8 and Standard 7, para. 15; Children's Rights and Business Principle 7. The phrase 'prompt, adequate, and effective compensation' is considered customary international law for the type of compensation owed in order to effect a lawful expropriation. See Annex A, 6. Note that the standards mentioned in this Guidance align with the commitments to zero tolerance for land displacements of any legitimate tenure rights recently taken by major food and beverage enterprises.

54. VGGT, 16.1 and 16.3; PRAI Principle 6.2.1; IFC Performance Standard 5, paras. 9-10, 12, 19, 27-28, and Performance Standard 7, paras 9 and 14. As per IFC Performance Standard 7, para. 14, land-based compensation should be provided in lieu of cash compensation where feasible and continued access to natural resources should be ensured or equivalent replacement resources identified. As a last option, cash compensation should be provided and alternative livelihoods should be identified.

55. CFS-RAI Principle 8.ii. See Annex A, 7.

56. Fundamental principles developed by the World Organisation for Animal Health (OIE). For further information, see the Farm Animal Welfare Council's Five Freedoms at www.fawc.org.uk/freedoms.htm.

57. England's regulations 2000 (S.I. 2000 No. 1870) and Regulation 3(1) on the welfare of farmed animals.

58. OECD Guidelines, VI.1; CFS-RAI Principle 10; VGGT 4.3, 11.2, 12.6 and 12.10; PRAI Principle 7; IFC Performance Standard 1.1.

59. A list of toxic substances can be found in: the list of hazardous agrochemicals of the World Health Organization (WHO); the WHO recommended classification of pesticides by hazard class Ia (extremely hazardous) or Ib (highly hazardous); the Stockholm Convention on Persistent Organic Pollutants (POPs) of 2004; the Rotterdam Convention on the prior informed consent procedure for certain hazardous chemicals and pesticides in international trade of 2004; the Basel Convention on the control of transboundary movements of hazardous wastes and their disposal of 1992; the Montreal Protocol on substances that deplete the ozone layer of 1999; and the list 'Substitute It Now' (SIN) for pesticides.

60. Although most instruments that have been endorsed through an intergovernmental process refer to 'resource use efficiency', the paragraph 9 on water consumption of IFC Performance Standard 3 goes further by requiring the enterprise to 'adopt measures that avoid or reduce water usage'.

61. IFC Performance Standard 6, para 20, defines legally protected area as an area that meets the definition of the *International Union for Conservation of Nature (IUCN)*: 'A clearly defined geographical space, recognised, dedicated and managed, through legal or other effective means, to achieve the long-term conservation of nature with associated ecosystem services and cultural values.' This includes areas proposed by governments for such designation.

62. OECD Guidelines, VI.6; CFS-RAI Principles 1.i and 6; PRAI Principle 7; IFC Performance Standards 3 and 6; CBD; Convention on international trade in endangered species or wild flora and fauna CITES of 1975. See also Annex A, 8.

63. OECD Guidelines, II.A.5 & 7, II.A.15, and VII; CFS-RAI Principle 9.i; VGGT, 6.9, 9.12 & 16.6; UN Global Compact Principle 10. See Annex A, 9.1. In addition, the International Standards on Combating Money Laundering and the Financing of Terrorism and Proliferation developed by the Financial Action Task Force and endorsed by 180 countries in 2003 are relevant for financial institutions. Preventive measures, including customer due diligence and record keeping, are particularly useful to combat corruption.

64. OECD Guidelines, XI.1-2. See Annex A, 9.2.

65. OECD Guidelines, X.2-3. See Annex A, 9.3.

66. The G20/OECD Principles of Corporate Governance are the international corporate governance benchmark for policy makers, investors, corporations and other stakeholders worldwide. They have been adopted as one of the Financial Stability Board's (FSB) key standards for sound financial systems and have been used by the World Bank Group in more than 60 country reviews worldwide. They serve as the basis for the guidelines on corporate governance of banks issued by the Basel Committee on Banking Supervision. *www.oecd.org/corporate/principles-corporate-governance.htm*.

67. OECD Guidelines, IX; CFS-RAI Principle 7, iv; ILO MNE Declaration, 19; CBD, Article 16; UN Global Compact Principle 9.

68. IFC Performance Standard 6, para. 26.

69. OECD Guidelines, IV, Commentary 44; UN Guiding Principles, para. 16.

70. The Commission of the Codex Alimentarius defines traceability as the ability to follow the movement of a food through specified stage(s) of production, processing and distribution.

71. *Mass balance traceability* controls the exact volume of assessed and certified material entering the supply chain. An equivalent volume of the product leaving the supply chain can be sold or certified. Certified and non-certified components may be mixed. *Physical segregation traceability* identifies and traces certified materials and products through the supply chain. *Chain of custody* refers to the chronological documentation or paper trail showing the seizure, custody, control, transfer, analysis, and disposition of physical product.

72. More information in this regard can be found in Annex A, 1.3.

73. For further information, you can refer to: Annex A, Section 1.5; IFC, 2009; and the OECD Due Diligence Guidance for Meaningful Stakeholder Engagement in the Extractive Sector.

74. As detailed in IISD guide to negotiating investment contracts (IISD, 2014), Environmental Impact Assessments (EIAs) are now firmly established practice for projects in a wide range of economic sectors. About two thirds of the approximately 110 developing countries had enacted some form of EIA legislation by the mid-1990s. Social Impact Assessments are less common but increasingly becoming part of EIA process and practice. Generally agreed-upon principles for social impact assessments are lacking, but the International Association for Impact Assessment has

published a coherent set of guidelines. Other variants include sustainability assessments that integrate social, economic and environmental perspectives or cumulative impact assessments. There is a growing practice of conducting environmental and social impact assessments together. Impact assessments may also cover impacts on animal welfare.

75. Risk analysis tools such as those developed by the World Wildlife Fund (WWF) can help identify risks. They include the supply risk analysis tool (*www.supplyrisk.org*) and the water risk filter (*http://waterriskfilter.panda.org*).

76. More information can be found in Annex A, 2 and 6.

77. For example, whether the financial service is primarily used to establish ownership over, finance or support the *general performance* of the client (e.g. general corporate loans or financing), or only its *specific performance* (e.g. project financing) may bear over the scope of the due diligence process recommended by the OECD Guidelines. In the first case, the financial institution is likely expected to respond to all adverse impacts associated with the activities of the client. In the last case, it may only be expected to respond to the impacts of the activities it finances or supports.

78. As per the UN Human Rights Office of the High Commissioner in *The Corporate Responsibility to Respect Human Rights, An Interpretive Guide,* remedy is not only the process of providing remedy for an adverse impact but also the substantive outcomes that can counteract, or make good, the adverse impact. These outcomes may take a range of forms, such as apologies, restitution, rehabilitation, financial or non-financial compensation, and punitive sanctions (whether criminal or administrative, such as fines), as well as the prevention of harm through, for example, injunctions or guarantees of non-repetition.

79. The programme undertaken by the Sustainability Initiative of South Africa (SIZA) offers a good example of a local social compliance programme. This ethical trading programme was developed by the local growers' association. It created a unifying set of standards for South Africa's fruit producers, based on domestic laws, the reference code and reference audit process and methodology of the Global Social Compliance Programme, and ILO conventions. The major retailer works with local organisations to build capacities. By empowering local counterparts, the retailer looks to ensure that its investments in the social performance of its agricultural supply chain in South Africa are sustainable.

80. Following the Rana Plaza disaster, the French NCP underlined the importance of independent and high-quality audits in the following report: NCP report on the Implementation of the OECD Guidelines in the Textile and Clothing Sector following a referral from Nicole Bricq, Minister of Foreign Trade, Recommendation #6 on pages 57-58, 2 December 2013, *www.tresor.economie.gouv.fr/File/398811*.

81. For instance, SGS has developed a Global Social Compliance Programme to reduce audit fatigue.

References

FAO (2014), *Innovation in Family Farming*, The State of Food and Agriculture, Food and Agriculture Organization, Rome.

FAO (2012), *Investing in Agriculture for a Better Future*, The State of Food and Agriculture, Food and Agriculture Organization, Rome.

IISD (2014), *Guide to Negotiating Investment Contracts for Farmland and Water*, International Institute for Sustainable Development, Manitoba.

OECD/FAO (2015), *OECD-FAO Agricultural Outlook 2015*, OECD Publishing, Paris, http://dx.doi.org/10.1787/agr_outlook-2015-en

OECD (2014), *Due Diligence in the Financial Sector: Adverse Impacts Directly Linked to Operations, Products or Services by a Business Relationship* http://mneguidelines.oecd.org/global-forum/GFRBC-2014-financial-sector-document-1.pdf.

OECD (2013), *OECD Due Diligence Guidance for Responsible Supply Chains of Minerals from Conflict-Affected and High-Risk Areas: Second Edition*, OECD Publishing, Paris, http://dx.doi.org/10.1787/9789264185050-en.

Annex A

Measures for risk mitigation and prevention along agricultural supply chains

This Annex identifies the risks of adverse impacts arising along agricultural supply chains and proposes measures to mitigate and prevent them, drawing from the same standards as the model enterprise policy. Proposed measures may reinforce each other. For instance, respecting labour rights, including by providing decent wages and working conditions, can support access to adequate food and help achieve the highest attainable standard of physical and mental health. The implementation of the proposed measures should be tailored to the position and the type of involvement of each enterprise in the supply chain, the context and location of its operations, as well as its size and capacities.

1. Cross-cutting RBC standards

1.1 Disclosure

Risks

A lack of transparency can create distrust and deprive enterprises of the possibility to resolve minor problems before they escalate into large conflicts, while maximum information sharing can reduce transaction costs for all stakeholders (FAO, 2010). Unless information is provided in a linguistically and culturally adequate, measurable, verifiable and timely manner, including through regular consultation meetings and the general media, enterprises run the risk of not being fully understood by potentially affected stakeholders or of failing to reach out to all relevant parties (IFC, 2012). In the absence of clear and enforceable laws on transparency and disclosure, enhanced due diligence is warranted (OECD, 2006).

Risk mitigation measures

- **Provide timely and accurate information** to the public, without endangering the competitive position or duties to beneficial owners of the enterprise, about:
  - purpose, nature, and scale of the operations
  - lease agreements and/or contracts and their terms
  - activities, structure, ownership and governance of the enterprise
  - financial situation and performance of the enterprise
  - RBC policies and implementation process, including the stakeholder engagement process and the availability of grievance and redress mechanisms

- environmental, Social and Human Rights Impact Assessments (ESHRIAs), including foreseeable risk factors, such as potential environmental, social, human rights, health and safety impacts of the enterprise's operations on various stakeholders as well as on sacred sites or lands and waters traditionally used or occupied by indigenous peoples and local communities
- environmental, social and human rights management plans and characteristics of products.[1]

- **Diffuse information** through all appropriate means of notification (print, electronic and social media, including newspapers, radio, television, mailings, local meetings, etc.), taking into account the situation of remote or isolated and largely non-literate communities and ensuring that such notification and consultation take place in the language(s) of the affected communities.[2]
- In the event of imminent threat to human health or the environment, **share immediately** and without delay all information which could enable authorities and the public to take measures to prevent or mitigate harm arising from the threat.[3]
- **Tailor disclosure policies** to the nature, size and location of the operations, with due regard taken of costs, business confidentiality and other competitive concerns.[4]

1.2 Consultations

Risks

A lack of consultations with stakeholders likely to be affected by the operations prevents enterprises from realistically assessing the project viability and from identifying effective and context-specific response measures. Inclusive and fully transparent consultations can lower transaction costs, reduce opposition and create trust among stakeholders.

Risk mitigation measures

- Develop and implement a **stakeholder engagement plan** tailored to the risks, impacts and development stage of the operations and to the characteristics and interests of affected communities. Where applicable, the plan should include differentiated measures to allow the effective participation of those identified as disadvantaged or vulnerable.[5]
- Hold early and ongoing good-faith, effective and meaningful **consultations with potentially affected communities**, with due regard for the international standards cited in Annex B. Such consultations should also be held for any modifications to the operations.[6]
- Organise consultation and decision-making processes **without intimidation**, in a climate of trust, prior to taking decisions, and respond to the contributions taking into consideration existing power imbalances between different parties.[7]
- Where necessary, strive to provide **technical and legal assistance** to affected communities to participate in project development in non-discriminatory ways, together with representative institutions of affected communities and in co-operation with these communities.

- Take **full and fair consideration of the views expressed** during the consultations, allow for sufficient time between notification and public consultation on proposed operations for affected communities to prepare their response, and inform those affected about how their concerns have been considered.[8]
- **Document and implement agreements** resulting from consultations, including by establishing a process by which community views and concerns can be properly recorded. While written statements may be preferred, the views of the community members could also be recorded on video or audio tape, or any other appropriate way, subject to the consent of communities.[9]
- To the extent possible, verify that **community representatives** do in fact represent the views of the stakeholders they represent and that they can be relied upon to faithfully communicate the results of consultations to their constituents.
- When carrying out **impact assessments**, establish mechanisms for the participation of the communities, including vulnerable groups, in designing and conducting the assessments, identify actors responsible for liability, redress, insurance and compensation, and establish a review and appeals process.[10]

1.3 Impact assessment

Risks

Enterprises can avoid or, when unavoidable, mitigate the actual and potential adverse impacts of their operations, processes, goods and services by assessing the risks of such impacts over their full life-cycle on an ongoing basis. Such assessments can allow them to develop a comprehensive and forward-looking approach to the management of risks, including the risks arising from the operations of their business partners.[11]

Risk mitigation measures

- Include in an impact assessment the **following stages**:
  1. Screening, i.e. determining which proposals should be subject to the impact assessment, to exclude those unlikely to have adverse impacts and to indicate the level of assessment required.
  2. Scoping, i.e. defining the focus of the impact assessment and key issues to be studied.
  3. Impact analysis.
  4. Identification of mitigation measures, including, as appropriate under the circumstances: not proceeding with the operations; finding alternatives to avoid adverse impacts; incorporating safeguards in the design of the operations; or providing monetary and/or non-monetary compensation for adverse impacts.
- Cover, as appropriate, the following **likely impacts** (it may be relevant to cover not only adverse impacts but also positive impacts in order to enhance the latter) when undertaking an environmental, social and human rights impact assessment (ESHRIA):
  - environmental impacts, such as those on soil, water, air, forest, and biodiversity[12]

- social impacts that may affect the well-being, vitality and viability of affected communities, including quality of life as measured in terms of income distribution, physical and social integrity and protection of individuals and communities, employment levels and opportunities, health and welfare, education, and availability and standards of housing and accommodation, infrastructure, services
- human rights impacts, that may affect for instance the enjoyment of the economic, social, cultural, civil and political rights of affected communities
- impacts on the cultural heritage, way of life, values, belief systems, language(s), customs, economy, relationships with the local environment and particular species, social organisation and traditions of affected communities
- impacts on women with due regard to their role as food providers, custodians of biodiversity and holders of traditional knowledge[13]
- impacts on animal welfare.

- Invite **affected communities** to be involved in conducting the impact assessment, solicit information from them, and provide them with regular feedback throughout all stages of the impact assessment.[14]
- Assess the risks and impacts in the context of the **project's area of influence** where the project involves physical elements, aspects, and facilities that are likely to generate impacts.[15]

1.4 Benefit sharing

Risks

To avoid the risk of creating local opposition and to reduce transaction costs, enterprises should explore ways to maximise the positive impacts of their operations on local communities. Engaging in consultations on the benefits of their operations among various stakeholders can build trust, help ensure local acceptance and create long-term alliances among parties while preventing conflict. Ensuring that operations benefit these stakeholders can also facilitate the identification of acceptable locations for operations and can draw on local knowledge to ensure an optimal use of the agro-ecological potential (FAO, 2010; UN, 2009).

Benefit sharing is separate (and may be additional) to compensation for unavoidable adverse impacts; it aims to build a partnership between the enterprise and indigenous peoples or local communities in recognition of their contribution to the operations. In specific circumstances, indigenous peoples or local communities may be entitled to share the benefits arising from operations if enterprises use their land, resources or knowledge.[16] Such benefits can be monetary or non-monetary[17] as agreed between the enterprise and the relevant community as part of the consultation process. The decision as regards the types of benefits can be informed by ESHRIAs.[18]

There are, however, also risks associated with benefit sharing. Enterprises face risks of conflict with indigenous peoples when, after negotiating benefit-sharing agreements, benefits are not actually shared with the whole community but captured by a specific group of stakeholders. Benefit sharing may be agreed with some, but not all, relevant communities, leading to the exclusion of certain communities. Such risks can be mitigated through meaningful stakeholder engagement in the due diligence process.

Risk mitigation measures

- Strive to **identify opportunities** for development benefits, such as through: the creation of local forward and backward linkages and of local jobs with safe working environments; the diversification of income-generating opportunities; capacity development; local procurement; technology transfer; improvements in local infrastructure; better access to credit and markets, particularly for small and medium-sized businesses; payments for environmental services; allocation of revenue; or the creation of trust funds.[19]
- Ensure that operations are **in line with the development priorities** and social objectives of the host government.[20]
- Share **monetary and non-monetary benefits** arising from operations involving indigenous peoples' lands, resources and knowledge, on the basis of the consultation process and ESHRIAs, in a way that does not unfairly benefit specific groups, but that fosters equitable and sustainable social development.[21]

1.5 Grievance mechanisms

Risks

Operational-level grievance mechanisms designed as early-warning risk-awareness systems offer a locally based, simplified, and mutually beneficial way to settle issues between enterprises and affected communities, including tenure rights holders, by helping resolve minor disputes quickly, inexpensively, and fairly before they are elevated to formal dispute resolution mechanisms, including judicial courts (IFC, 2009). They can provide valuable feedback to enterprises by: serving as an early warning system for larger problems; yielding insights from individuals that spotlight opportunities for improvement in company operations or management systems; and indicating possible systemic changes to ensure particular grievances do not recur (CAO, 2008).

Risk mitigation measures

- **Scale** the grievance mechanism according to the risks and adverse impacts of the operations, with a view to seeking to resolve concerns promptly, using an understandable, transparent, culturally appropriate and readily accessible consultative process, without retribution to the party that originated the issue or concern.[22]
- **Engage with affected stakeholders** about the mechanism design and performance to ensure that: it meets their needs; they will use it in practice; and there is a shared interest in ensuring its success.[23]
- Avoid using grievance mechanisms established by enterprises to **preclude access** to judicial or non-judicial grievance mechanisms, including the NCPs under the OECD Guidelines, or to undermine the role of trade unions in addressing labour-related disputes.[24]

In addition, the effectiveness criteria for non-judicial grievance mechanisms contained in the UN Guiding Principles (Principle 31) provide an important reference point: non-judicial grievance mechanisms, both state-based and non-state-based, should follow the criteria detailed in Table A.1 to be effective.

Table A.1. **Characteristics of effective grievance mechanisms**

Legitimate	Enable trust from the stakeholder groups for whose use they are intended, and be accountable for the fair conduct of grievance processes.
Accessible	Be known to all stakeholder groups for whose use they are intended, and provide adequate assistance for those who may face particular barriers to access.
Predictable	Provide a clear and known procedure with an indicative time frame for each stage, and clarity on the types of process and outcome available and means of monitoring implementation.
Equitable	Seek to ensure that aggrieved parties have reasonable access to sources of information, advice and expertise necessary to engage in a grievance process on fair, informed and respectful terms.
Transparent	Keep parties to a grievance informed about its progress, and provide sufficient information about the mechanism's performance to build confidence in its effectiveness and meet any public interest at stake.
Rights-compatible	Ensure that outcomes and remedies accord with internationally recognised human rights.
A source of continuous learning	Draw on relevant measures to identify lessons for improving the mechanism and preventing future grievances and harms.
Based on engagement and dialogue	Consult the stakeholder groups for whose use they are intended on their design and performance, and focus on dialogue as the means to address and resolve grievances.

Source: UN Guiding Principles, Principle 31.

2. Human rights

Risks

Enterprises run the risk of not respecting human rights when they cause or contribute to adverse human rights impacts within the context of their own activities and fail to address such impacts when they occur. They should prevent or mitigate adverse human rights impacts that are directly linked to their business operations, products or services by a business relationship.[25] The corporate responsibility to respect human rights exists independently of states' abilities and/or willingness to fulfil their own human rights obligations and does not diminish these obligations.[26] If national laws are not sufficiently developed or enforced, enterprises should use enhanced due diligence in identifying and addressing the risk of adverse human rights impacts.

The interdependence of all human rights, including economic, social, cultural, civil and political rights, should be borne in mind. Enterprises should regularly review their responsibilities related to human rights to qualitatively understand if they may not be respecting human rights, including those that are not specifically addressed in this Guidance.

Risk mitigation measures

- **Identify right holders** potentially affected by the operations of the enterprise and its business partners. This generally entails undertaking an in-depth fact-finding review of the enterprise's actual or potential operations and relationships, and then qualitatively evaluating those operations against human rights standards to identify actors whose rights may be affected. Proactive consultations with relevant stakeholders are necessary to fully understand all the potential adverse impacts of the enterprise's operations and relationships.[27]
- **Carry out human rights due diligence** by assessing actual and potential human rights impacts,[28] integrating and acting upon the findings, tracking responses, and communicating how impacts are addressed. Human rights due diligence is an on-going exercise, recognising that human rights risks may change over time as the operations and operating context evolve.[29]
- Ensure that **all stakeholders involved are treated fairly**, particularly groups in vulnerable situations such as women, youth, and minorities, recognising their respective situations, constraints and needs.[30]
- Recognise the vital role played by women in agriculture and take appropriate measures to eliminate **discrimination against women** and to help ensure their full professional development and advancement,[31] including by facilitating equal access and control over natural resources, inputs, productive tools, advisory and financial services, training, markets and information.[32]

3. Labour rights

Risks

Enterprises can bring substantial benefits to host countries and societies by contributing to economic and social welfare through improving living standards and creating attractive employment opportunities, and by facilitating the enjoyment of human rights and labour rights. In addition to ensuring core labour standards for their own workers, they can help improve the working conditions of informal workers, including in subsistence farms.

States Parties to the International Covenant on Economic, Social and Cultural Rights (ICESCR) recognise the rights to the enjoyment of just and favourable conditions of work (Article 7) and to form trade unions (Article 8). The International Covenant on Civil and Political Rights (ICCPR) also protects the right to form and join trade unions. International labour conventions[33] also address work-related rights.[34] While human rights treaties such as the ICESCR and ICCPR are addressed to states, enterprises may negatively impact the enjoyment of the rights they contain. Thus, they have an important role to play in supporting the progressive realisation of these rights. Respecting the labour rights contained in these conventions, including the eight fundamental ILO conventions, can help enterprises minimise negative impacts and maximise positive impacts. For instance, establishing a genuine dialogue with freely chosen workers' representatives enables both workers and employers to better understand each other's challenges and find ways to resolve them (ILO, 2006).

However, respecting labour rights in the agricultural sector may be a challenge, as both independent and waged employment often remains informal, and many agricultural workers are excluded from the scope of labour laws (UN, 2009). 60% of child labourers aged 5-17 work in agriculture (ILO, 2011a). The working and living conditions of plantation workers have also been a continued source of concern, notably compulsory pregnancy testing, debt bondage, and health risks linked to the widespread misuse of pesticides (UN, 2009).

Marginalised groups, such as women, youth and indigenous and migrant workers, as well as workers employed on a casual, piecework or seasonal basis, and informal workers, often face abusive or insalubrious working conditions (UN, 2009). The situation of women raises specific risks: in developing countries, 43% of the agricultural labour force is composed of women but the agro-industry tends to code female tasks as unskilled, employ women for labour-intensive tasks and pay them less than men with fewer opportunities for advancement (ILO, 2011b).

Violations of core labour rights may encourage disruptive social tensions that may affect the enterprise's performance. An enterprise using discriminatory employment and occupation practices limits its access to talents from a wider pool of skills and competencies. The sense of injustice and resentment generated by discrimination is likely to affect workers' performance (ILO, 2008).

Risk mitigation measures[35]

Workers' protection

- Be guided throughout operations by **the principle of equality of opportunity and treatment in employment** and do not discriminate against workers with respect to employment or occupation on such grounds as race, colour, sexual orientation or gender identity, religion, political opinion, national extraction or social origin, or other status, unless selectivity concerning worker characteristics furthers established governmental policies that specifically promote greater equality of employment opportunity or relates to the inherent requirements of a job; make qualifications, skill and experience the basis for the recruitment, placement, training and advancement of staff at all levels.[36]
- Respect the **minimum age** for admission to employment or work in order to secure the effective abolition of child labour.[37]
- Refrain from employing or benefitting from **forced labour**, which consists of any work or service not voluntarily performed that is exacted from an individual under threat of force or penalty.
- **Monitor** the primary supply chain on an ongoing basis in order to identify any significant changes or new risks or incidents of child and/or forced labour, and work with primary suppliers to take corrective action and remedy them.[38]

Decent working conditions

- Observe **standards of employment** and industrial relations not less favourable than those observed by comparable employers. Where comparable employers may not exist in the country in which the enterprise operates, provide the best possible wages, benefits and conditions of work within the framework of government policies. These should be at least adequate to satisfy the basic needs of the workers and their families.[39]

- Endeavour to provide **stable employment** for workers, and observe freely negotiated obligations concerning employment stability and social security.[40]

- In considering changes in operations that would have major employment effects, provide **reasonable notice of such changes** to workers' representatives, and, where appropriate, to the relevant governmental authorities, and co-operate with them to mitigate to the maximum extent practicable adverse effects.[41]

Workers' representation and collective bargaining

- Recognise the importance of a **climate of mutual understanding and confidence** that is favourable to the aspirations of the workers.[42]

- Recognise that workers, without discrimination whatsoever, have the right to **establish and join organisations** of their own choosing without previous authorisation.

- Establish systems for regular **consultation and co-operation** between employers and workers and their representatives on matters of mutual concern, as well as with competent authorities to ensure adherence to national social development policies.

- Establish systems to provide regular **information** to workers and their representatives to support meaningful negotiations on employment conditions and to enable them to obtain a true and fair view of the enterprise performance.[43]

- Refrain from **discriminatory or disciplinary action** against workers who make bona fide reports to management or, as appropriate to the competent public authorities on practices that contravene the law, the OECD Guidelines, or the enterprise's policies.

- Do not threaten to **transfer** the whole or part of an operating unit from the country concerned or to transfer workers from the component entities in other countries in order to influence unfairly negotiations with workers' representatives or to hinder the exercise of workers' right to organise.

- Do not retaliate, interfere with or discriminate against **workers' representatives.**[44]

- Enable authorised workers' representatives to negotiate on **collective bargaining or labour management relations**.

- Include in collective agreements provisions for the **settlement of disputes** arising over their interpretation and application and for ensuring mutually respected rights and responsibilities.[45]

Local employment

- To the greatest extent practicable and without discrimination, **employ local workers**, including in managerial positions, and provide training with a view to improving skill levels, in co-operation with workers' representatives and, where appropriate, relevant governmental authorities.[46]

Training

- Ensure that **relevant training** is provided to workers at all levels to meet the needs of the operations, where appropriate, in co-operation with relevant governmental authorities and employers' and workers' organisations. Such training should, to the extent possible, develop generally useful skills and promote career opportunities.

- When operating in developing countries, participate in programmes encouraged by governments and supported by employers' and workers' organisations that aim to encourage **skill formation** and development and to provide vocational guidance.[47]
- Provide appropriate training, education and mentorship programmes for **youth** to increase their capacity and/or access to decent work and entrepreneurship, and promote access to training by women.[48]
- Wherever feasible, **make the services of skilled resource personnel available** to help in training programmes organised by governments as part of a contribution to national development.[49]

4. Health and safety

Risks

Agricultural activities often involve some of the most hazardous activities for workers and many agricultural workers suffer from occupational accidents and illnesses. Exposure to bad weather, close contact with dangerous animals or plants, extensive use of chemical products, difficult working postures and lengthy hours, and the use of hazardous tools and machinery all lead to health problems (IFPRI, 2006). For instance, the estimated number of pesticide poisonings ranges between 2 and 5 million per year, of which 40 000 are fatal (ILO, 2005 and 2011b). Land use changes, the loss of natural buffer areas, such as wetlands, mangroves, and upland forests that mitigate the effects of natural hazards (flooding, landslides, and fire), or the diminution or degradation of natural resources, including decreasing quality, quantity, and availability of freshwater, may result in increased vulnerability and community safety-related impacts (IFC, 2012).

Human health can be at risk with unsafe levels of biological, chemical or physical hazards in food. These hazards originate from the environment (e.g. toxic metals, dioxins and naturally occurring toxins), agricultural practices (e.g. residues of veterinary drugs and pesticides), or a poor handling of product (e.g. pathogenic molds). Physical hazards include filth, pests, hair, or plastic. Food safety management systems, including a complete 'farm to fork' control system that incorporates biosecurity measures and the use of safe water, can prevent these risks.

Human health is also closely linked to animal health. The "One Health" concept is founded on an awareness of the major opportunities that exist to protect public health through policies aimed at preventing and controlling pathogens at the level of animal populations, at the interface between humans, animals and the environment. This concept has been endorsed by several governments and led to measures aiming to prevent diseases affecting both people and animals and to ensure a responsible use of antibiotics for both.[50] 60% of the pathogens that cause infectious diseases in humans are of animal origin. These diseases, known as zoonoses, can be transmitted by domestic or wild animals. Animal diseases that are transmissible to humans present a public health risk worldwide. An effective and economical solution to protect humans is to combat all zoonotic pathogens through their control at the animal source.

The ICESCR provides for the progressive realisation of the right to the enjoyment of the highest attainable standard of physical and mental health (Article 12). The Committee on Economic, Social and Cultural Rights[51] interprets this right as 'an inclusive right extending not only to timely and appropriate health care but also to the underlying determinants of health, such as access to safe and potable water and adequate sanitation, an adequate supply of safe food, nutrition and housing, healthy occupational and environmental conditions, and access to health-related education and information'. The Committee states that 'the right to health, like all human rights, imposes three types or levels of obligations on States Parties: the obligations to respect, protect and fulfil. In turn, the obligation to fulfil contains obligations to facilitate, provide and promote.'[52]

While human rights treaties such as the ICESCR are addressed to states, enterprises may negatively impact the progressive realisation of the right to the enjoyment of the highest attainable standard of physical and mental health or undermine State Party actions to progressively realise it. Thus, they have an important role to play in supporting the progressive realisation of this right. In addition to the direct health risks detailed above, agricultural operations and food systems may affect individuals' health more indirectly.

Risk mitigation measures[53]

- Evaluate the **risks and impacts** to the health and safety of the affected communities throughout the operations.
- Establish **preventive and control measures** that are consistent with good international industry practice,[54] and commensurate with the nature and magnitude of the identified risks and impacts, trying to avoid, and, if unsuccessful, to minimise risks and impacts.
- Avoid or minimise workers, third party and community exposure to **hazardous materials and substances** that may be released by the operations, including by modifying, substituting, or eliminating the condition or material causing the potential hazards, and by exercising reasonable efforts to control the safety of deliveries, transportation and disposal of hazardous materials and wastes.
- Avoid or minimise the potential for community exposure to water-borne, water-based, water-related, vector-borne and communicable **diseases** that could result from operations, taking into consideration differentiated exposure to and higher sensitivity of vulnerable groups.
- Assist and collaborate with affected communities, local government agencies, and other relevant parties, in their preparations to respond effectively to **emergency situations**, especially when their participation and collaboration are necessary to respond to such emergency situations.[55]
- Consider observing global **food safety standards**, such as the Codex Alimentarius,[56] and global animal health standards, such as OIE standards.[57]
- Promote traceability to ensure food safety but also to facilitate social and environmental management and increase trust.[58]

5. Food security and nutrition

Risks

Under the ICESCR (Article 11), adequate food is part of the right to an adequate standard of living.[59] The States Parties to the ICESCR undertake to take steps to progressively realise the right to an adequate standard of living, including adequate food.

The ICESCR also recognises the fundamental right of everyone to be free from hunger. Recognising this right, States Parties should consider taking the measures needed to improve methods of food production, conservation and distribution and taking into account the problems of both food-importing and food-exporting countries. The Committee on Economic, Social and Cultural Rights has interpreted these rights to be realised 'when every man, woman and child, alone or in community with others, have physical and economic access at all times to adequate food or means for its procurement.' It states that 'the right to adequate food, like any other human right, imposes three types or levels of obligations on States Parties: the obligations to respect, to protect and to fulfil' and that 'as part of their obligations to protect people's resource base for food, States Parties should take appropriate steps to ensure that activities of the private business sector and civil society are in conformity with the right to food'.[60]

The FAO Voluntary Guidelines to support the progressive realisation of the right to adequate food in the context of national food security provide guidance to governments in realising the right to adequate food, which may include promoting the availability of food in a quantity and of a quality sufficient to satisfy the dietary needs of individuals, as well as the physical and economic accessibility to adequate food, free from unsafe substances and acceptable within a given culture, or the means of its procurement. The Guidelines encourage governments to take measures to ensure that all food, whether locally produced or imported, freely available or sold on markets, is safe and consistent with national food safety standards. They also suggest that governments establish comprehensive and rational food-control systems that reduce the risk of food-borne disease using risk analysis and supervisory mechanisms to ensure food safety in the entire food chain, including animal feed.

While the FAO Voluntary Guidelines are addressed to states, enterprises have an important role to play. Agricultural investments have increased following food price hikes in 2008, particularly to respond to a growing demand for food - it is estimated that global food production will need to increase by 60% by 2050 in order to meet projected demand. While such investments hold the promise of increasing production, reducing poverty, and fostering economic development, they may also undermine access to food in various ways. One of the most prominent adverse impacts can result from acquiring large tracts of land and, in the process, displacing communities from it, or hindering their access to it (FAO, 2010).

Risk mitigation measures

- To the extent possible, **consider the impacts of operations** on the availability and access to food, local employment, dietary preferences and stability of food supply, including by involving local governments and other relevant stakeholders.
- When appropriate, **identify food-related concerns** of different stakeholders and evaluate strategies for meeting investment objectives while respecting the food-related concerns of different stakeholders, through consultations with relevant stakeholders.
- To the extent possible, **adjust project design** to address concerns about negative impacts on food security and nutrition, by for instance: considering feasible alternative investments if proposed investments lead to the physical and/or economic displacement of local communities; reclaiming degraded lands or choosing land that has not been previously used for agriculture yet is not environmentally sensitive; or improving

agricultural productivity through sustainable intensification in order to contribute to food security and nutrition.

- To the extent possible, **consider contributing** to improving access to food and the resilience and nutrition[61] of local populations by: increasing the production of safe, nutritious and diverse foods and promoting the nutritional value of food and agricultural products; facilitating access to inputs, technology, and markets; generating employment in downstream activities; or setting up community storage facilities to reduce post-harvest losses and price volatility.[62]

6. Tenure rights over and access to natural resources

Risks

Land tenure risk, arising when several land claims overlap, represents a statistically significant risk in concession investments in emerging economies (Munden Project, 2013). Indeed, among 39 large-scale agri-business investments analysed by the World Bank and UNCTAD, land tenure was identified as the most common cause of grievances for affected communities, particularly due to disputes over land over which communities had informal land use rights and to a lack of transparency, especially on conditions and process for land acquisition (WB, 2014). In 2013, half of the issues raised in letters of complaints received by the IFC and MIGA Compliance Advisor Ombudsman (CAO)[63] related to land. In addition, since 2000, nearly a quarter of all cases handled by the CAO have had both a land and a water component. Increased pressure on these resources leads to concerns over their access, quantity, and management, and both land and water are often entwined with a sense of culture and identity. In CAO's land-related complaints, the dominant grievances raised by individuals are land acquisition (22%), compensation (33%), and resettlement (32%) (CAO, 2013).

The food and beverage industry is second only to the extractive industry in being the recipient of accusations from civil society organisations for failing to give adequate consideration to rights related to access to land and water (EC, 2011).[64] Land should not be perceived solely as a productive asset. Its environmental and socio-cultural roles should be recognised as well; land can be a source of various ecosystem services, including drinking and irrigation water, and a safety net and an old age insurance for farmers. Land can also play a major role in the social, cultural or religious practices of indigenous peoples and local communities.

Although states have the primary responsibility to protect tenure rights, enterprises should assume that the legal framework may not always be adequate. Indeed, an estimated 70% of the land ownership units in developing countries are not formally registered (UN HABITAT, 2015; McDermott *et al.*, 2015). Thus, enterprises should ensure proactively that they respect legitimate tenure rights. In particular, the following risks should be considered:

- Risks arise when national laws do not reflect the full extent of legitimate tenure rights or when such laws are not implemented effectively. For instance, national land titling and registration systems may be inadequate, failing to protect the tenure rights of land users, particularly women, and providing enterprises with incomplete information regarding relevant land claims. Land tenure rights can be complicated further when the land is used only seasonally and may appear unused, for instance if it has been abandoned by internally displaced persons or if it is used for pasture, forage or shifting agriculture. Enterprises may then exclude from consultations certain right holders (whether statutory or customary, primary or secondary, formal or informal groups or individuals) that may be adversely affected by their activities (OECD, 2011).

- Risks may augment if states do not provide clear and transparent rules for consultations between enterprises and stakeholders, or safeguards to protect existing tenure rights from risks arising from large-scale transactions in tenure rights. In particular, enterprises may be at risk if national rules are not implemented or not sufficient to: (i) ensure appropriate engagement in good faith and in a culturally appropriate manner with the holders of tenure rights, and (ii) identify the modalities under which land and other natural resources will be transferred and used, including through the use of independent and participatory ex-ante and ex-post impact assessments, and/or the modalities to obtain redress (UN, 2009). A lack of inclusiveness in consultations over land acquisitions may cause tensions and possibly conflicts between enterprises and communities, which may feel excluded from the process and contest enterprises' rights (FAO, 2013).

- While governments hold the primary responsibility for providing prompt, adequate and effective compensation to former legitimate land tenure rights holders when expropriating land, enterprises have responsibilities to ensure that their operations do not lead to the resettlement of local communities without meaningful consultations or their forced evictions without proper compensation. As per the VGGT, states should expropriate only where land rights are required for a public purpose and should clearly define the concept of public purpose in law in order to allow for judicial review. However, in many developing countries, the unclear and/or broad definition of public purpose, the lack of land use plans, high corruption levels in land management and land speculation, lead to unlawful expropriation. Such expropriation may precipitate the loss of the livelihoods of local communities, or more limited access to land and other key natural resources, thus resulting in nutritional deprivation, social polarisation, entrenched poverty or political instability.[65] Thus, it may impede access to adequate food. Such expropriation may also infringe on the rights of indigenous peoples as set out in the UN Declaration on the Rights of Indigenous Peoples. Enterprises may be negatively impacted in their reputation and operations if they are connected to an expropriation for which the government has not undertaken appropriate consultations with local communities or obtained the free, prior, and informed consent of indigenous peoples and not provided due compensation. This is likely to cause tensions and conflicts between enterprises and communities that feel excluded or unfairly treated (FAO, 2013). In such cases, enterprises should consider options to withdraw from planned operations.

The level of land tenure risks depends on the type of investments. For greenfield investments, thorough due diligence should be undertaken to ensure that communities have not been expropriated for private purposes and without fair and prompt compensation. In the case of brownfield investments, joint ventures and mergers and acquisitions, previous operators may have been granted land tenure rights and land disputes may be inherited. Consequently, due diligence should ensure that the acquisition of these rights respected the standards set out in this Guidance, particularly as the VGGT were endorsed only in 2012. Investing in existing projects provides enterprises with an opportunity to ensure that land tenure rights were properly acquired, and if not to find ways to compensate affected stakeholders, and to re-engage with local communities to explore new partnership models.

Risk mitigation measures

- **Identify rights holders** - who consist not only of holders of officially recognised tenure rights, but also of public, private, communal, collective, indigenous and customary tenure rights that may not have been officially registered and titled, including women's tenure rights - and other relevant stakeholders, including through local and open consultations.[66]

- **Establish a committee** representative of the relevant stakeholders to advise on impact assessments, particularly on initial phases (screening and scoping) and on management, monitoring and contingency plans. Special consideration should be given to ensuring the adequate representation of indigenous peoples, local communities and marginalised groups.[67]

- Consider feasible alternative investments if proposed investments lead to the **physical and/or economic displacement** of local communities, recognising that states should expropriate only where rights to land, fisheries or forests are required for a public purpose and that they should clearly define the concept of public purpose in law.[68]

- When tenure right holders are negatively impacted by operations, work with the government to ensure that tenure rights holders receive a fair, prompt and appropriate **compensation** for those tenure rights negatively impacted by the operations by:
  - holding good-faith, effective and meaningful consultations on the compensation offered and ensuring consistent and transparent application of compensation standards
  - giving preference to land-based compensation, that is commensurate in quality, size and value, and otherwise providing compensation at full replacement cost for lost assets - including assets other than land (crops, water resources, irrigation infrastructure and land improvements) - and other assistance to help them improve or restore their standard of living or livelihoods
  - monitoring the implementation of the compensation arrangement.[69]

- Where government capacity is limited, play an active role in the resettlement planning, implementation and monitoring.[70]

7. Animal welfare

Risks

Significant animal welfare risks may arise in agricultural supply chains. They can be associated with limitations on space in individual stalls restricting the movement of animals, high stocking densities in groups increasing the potential for disease transmission and injurious contact with others, barren/unchanging environments leading to behavioural problems, feeding diets that do not satisfy hunger, injurious husbandry procedures that cause pain, and breeding for production traits that heighten anatomical or metabolic disorders. Inadequate inputs from knowledgeable and skilled stockpersons may increase these risks (IFC, 2014).

Improving animal welfare can make business sense. Disease is a good example of a joint threat to animal welfare and business sustainability. The OIE estimates that morbidity and mortality due to animal diseases cause the loss of at least 20% of livestock production globally – which represents at least 60 million tonnes of meat and 150 million tonnes of milk with a value of approximately USD 300 billion per year. In addition, affluence in many parts of the world has increased consumer choices and heightened expectations about food production standards. Surveys in Europe and North America found that the majority of consumers care about animal welfare and report a willingness to pay significantly more for animal products they perceive to have come from farm animals raised humanely (IFC, 2014).

References to animal welfare in international standards and principles are scarce. The most comprehensive guiding principles are developed by the World Organisation for Animal Health (OIE). In 2008, the members of the OIE adopted a definition of animal welfare in order to clarify on an international scale what it actually involves.[71] Animal welfare can be compromised in any size of farms when conditions and/or management are inadequate (RSPCA, 2014).

The nine OIE standards address specific welfare challenges, including the transport and slaughter of animals, production systems for cattle and poultry, the control of stray dog populations and the use of animals in research. These standards are based on scientific evidence and the fundamental principles for animal welfare are known as the 'five freedoms': freedom from hunger, thirst and malnutrition, from physical and thermal discomfort, from pain, injury and disease, from fear and distress, and to express normal patterns of behaviour.[72] The United Kingdom Department for Environment Food and Rural Affairs (DEFRA) offers an example of good practice by establishing these five freedoms. As underlined in the preface to DEFRA's code of recommendations for the welfare of livestock, enterprises engaged in animal production should demonstrate: caring and responsible planning and management; skilled, knowledgeable and conscientious stockmanship; appropriate environmental design; considerate handling, transport, and humane slaughter of animals (DEFRA, 2003).

In addition to OIE standards, the European Union (EU) has adopted a detailed set of animal welfare legislation, and Article 13 of the Treaty on the Functioning of the European Union recognises animals as 'sentient beings'.[73] While most EU rules on animal welfare apply only to EU producers, third countries wishing to export meat into the EU are required to establish standards equivalent with EU standards on welfare at the time of slaughter. Furthermore, the EU is working to bring convergence in global standards on animal welfare through international trade agreements. Additional standards and certification schemes on animal welfare have been developed by private enterprises, governments and civil society organisations.[74]

Risk mitigation measures

- Assess actual and potential impacts on animal welfare, using the framework of the **'Five Freedoms'**.
- Ensure that the **physical environment** allows comfortable resting, safe and comfortable movement, including normal postural changes, and the opportunity to perform types of natural behaviour that animals are motivated to perform.
- Ensure that animals have **access to sufficient feed and water**, suited to their age and needs, to maintain normal health and productivity and to prevent prolonged hunger, thirst, malnutrition or dehydration.

- When **painful procedures** cannot be avoided, manage the resulting pain to the extent that available methods allow.
- Ensure that the **handling of animals** fosters a positive relationship between humans and animals and does not cause injury, panic, lasting fear or avoidable stress.
- Use **livestock breeds** appropriate to the environment and circumstances so that they can be reared without production diseases and other intrinsic problems.[75]

8. Environmental protection and sustainable use of natural resources

Risks

Agricultural activities can deploy environmentally-friendly practices that can enhance ecosystem services, in particular by employing land management techniques conserving soil and moisture, protecting watersheds, restoring vegetation and habitat, and maintaining biodiversity. However, agricultural investments intended to increase agricultural production in the short term may also lead to ecosystem degradation in the long term, including land degradation, water resource depletion, and losses of pristine forests and biodiversity. An estimated 55-80% of global forest loss is due to land conversion for agricultural use (UNEP, 2015). The most commonly arising issues among the 39 investments analysed by the World Bank and UNCTAD in 2014 were related to agrochemical use, such as water contamination, chemical drift, and aerial spraying. In addition, agricultural activities can generate external impacts, including greenhouse gas emissions, impacts on watersheds, or deforestation occurring far from the location of the operations but directly linked to them (FAO, 2010).

Adverse environmental impacts may be due to the lack of proper environmental impact assessment prior to the investment and the absence of an effective environmental management system during its implementation (FAO, 2011). The quality, comprehensiveness and public availability of these assessments have often been the object of criticism of large-scale investments (FAO, 2010). Risks are higher when scientific evidence is not sufficient to fully assess adverse impacts. Risks for enterprises are also rapidly evolving as international standards on efficient resource utilisation and recycling, emission reduction, substitution or reduction of use of toxic substances, and biodiversity conservation advance (OECD, 2011; IFC, 2012).

Risk mitigation measures

- Establish and maintain a **system of environmental management** appropriate to the characteristics of the enterprise, including by: collecting and evaluating adequate and timely information regarding the environmental, health, and safety impacts of its activities; establishing measurable objectives and, where appropriate, targets for improved environmental performance and resource utilisation, including by developing an integrated pest and/or fertiliser management plan;[76] and regularly monitoring and verifying progress toward environmental, health, and safety objectives or targets.[77]
- Establish procedures to **monitor** and measure the effectiveness of the environmental management system. Where the government or third party has the responsibility for managing specific environmental risks and impacts and associated mitigation measures, collaborate in establishing and monitoring such mitigation measures. Where appropriate, consider involving representatives from affected communities to participate in monitoring activities.[78]

- **Address** the foreseeable environmental, health, and safety-related impacts associated with the processes, goods and services of the enterprise over their full life cycle with a view to avoiding or, when unavoidable, mitigating them. Where the proposed activities may have significant environmental, health, or safety impacts, and where they are subject to a decision of a competent authority, prepare an appropriate environmental impact assessment.[79]

- Where there is a risk of harm to the environment, avoid reference to the **lack of full scientific evidence** as a reason for postponing cost-effective measures to prevent or minimise such damage, consistent with the scientific and technical understanding of the risks, taking into account risks to human health and safety.[80]

- Maintain **contingency plans** for preventing, mitigating, and controlling serious environmental and health damage from the operations, including accidents and emergencies, and, where applicable, assist and collaborate with potentially affected communities and local government agencies to respond effectively to emergency situations, including by setting up mechanisms for immediate reporting to competent authorities.[81]

- Taking into account concerns about cost, business confidentiality, and the protection of intellectual property rights, provide the public and workers with adequate, measureable and timely **information** on the potential environmental, health and safety impacts of the activities of the enterprise, and engage in adequate and timely communication and consultation with the communities directly affected by the environmental, health and safety policies of the enterprise and by their implementation. [82]

- Seek to avoid negative impacts on, and support the conservation of **biodiversity, genetic resources and ecosystem services**, and when avoidance of such impacts is not possible, implement measures to minimise impacts and restore biodiversity and ecosystem services through an adaptive management approach.[83]

- Select the most appropriate production system, in collaboration with the government if appropriate, to enhance **resource use efficiency** while preserving the future availability of current resources.[84] This implies in particular striving to:

  - Improve **water conservation,** waste-water treatment and water use efficiency, and invest in and use technologies to achieve this objective.[85]

  - Improve the management of **agricultural inputs and outputs** to enhance the efficiency of production and minimise threats to the environment and to plant, animal and human health.[86]

  - Reduce **waste and losses** in production and post-harvest operations and enhance the productive use of waste and/or by-products.[87]

  - Implement technically and financially feasible and cost effective measures for improving efficiency in **energy consumption**.[88]

  - Take measures, as appropriate, to reduce and/or remove **greenhouse gas emissions**.[89]

9. Governance

9.1 Corruption

Risks

If the government does not have clear and well-enforced laws on transparency and anti-corruption, governance-related risks for enterprises are high (OECD, 2006). Government bodies overseeing the land sector are among the public entities most affected by service-level bribery, with only the police and the judiciary having higher levels of bribery (TI, 2011). Enterprises may have to offer undue advantages to obtain access to large land areas to the detriment of local communities holding customary land rights. Corruption may also affect the allocation of government-subsidised credit, with unnecessary fees being garnered by government officials when granting credits. Corruption can also increase the price of agricultural inputs, as agricultural input companies can sell their products to government agencies at an elevated price to provide public officials with a share of the profit.

Allegations of corruption either reduce the benefits of agricultural investment or prevent them from being realised by augmenting the cost of accessing resources, minimising synergies with current and future infrastructure development, and increasing the potential for conflict (FAO, 2010). They can undermine the confidence and trust of local communities in the enterprise, which are essential for developing positive relationships in the long term.

Risk mitigation measures

- Refrain from seeking or accepting exemptions not contemplated in the statutory or regulatory framework related to human rights, environment, health, safety, labour, taxation, or other issues.
- Avoid directly or indirectly (via a third party) offering, promising, giving, or demanding a bribe or other undue advantage to public officials, the workers of business partners or to their relatives or business associates, to obtain or retain business or any other improper advantage.
- Develop and adopt adequate internal controls, ethics and compliance programmes or measures for preventing and detecting bribery.
- Prohibit or discourage, in internal company controls, ethics and compliance programmes or measures, the use of small facilitation payments, which are generally illegal in the countries where they are made, and, if and when such payments are made, accurately record these in books and financial records.
- Ensure properly documented due diligence pertaining to the hiring of agents, ensure their appropriate and regular oversight, and ensure that their remuneration is appropriate and for legitimate services only.
- Abstain from any improper involvement in local political activities.[90]
- Use objectively assessed values, transparent and decentralised processes and services, and a right to appeal, to prevent corruption with regard to tenure rights, in particular the customary tenure rights of indigenous peoples and local communities.[91]

- Collaborate in the efforts by governments to implement the **OECD Convention** on Combating Bribery of Foreign Public Officials in International Business Transactions (OECD Anti-Bribery Convention).[92]

9.2 Taxation

Risks

Enterprises can contribute to the economic development of host countries by making timely payment of their tax liabilities. Tax governance and compliance in their risk management systems can ensure that financial, regulatory and reputational risks associated with taxation are fully identified and evaluated (OECD, 2011). As demonstrated by recent campaigns targeting large enterprises, tax avoidance can increase reputational risk.

Risk mitigation measures

- Provide authorities with **timely information** that is relevant or required by law for the purposes of the correct determination of taxes to be assessed in connection with operations.
- Conform **transfer pricing** practices to the arm's length principle.
- Adopt **risk management strategies** to ensure that the financial, regulatory and reputational risks associated with taxation are fully identified and evaluated.[93]

9.3 Competition

Risks

Anti-competitive practices may not only negatively affect consumers but also weaken the bargaining power of smallholders if excessive buyer power goes unchecked, thereby affecting food security and nutrition (UN, 2009). Similarly, dumping by large enterprises selling a product at loss in a competitive market can force competitors, including small and medium enterprises, out of the market. In countries where competition laws and regulations are not sufficiently developed or enforced, enterprises run the risk of infringing competition standards if they do not exercise heightened managerial care in refraining from practices that constitute an undue exercise of buyer power, such as retrospective reduction in prices without reasonable notification or unjustified payments imposed on supplier for consumer complaints (OECD, 2006).

Risk mitigation measures

- Refrain from entering into or carrying out **anti-competitive agreements** among competitors.
- **Co-operate with investigating competition authorities,** including by, subject to applicable law and appropriate safeguards, providing responses as promptly and completely as practicable to requests for information, and considering the use of available instruments, such as waivers of confidentiality where appropriate, to promote effective and efficient co-operation among investigating authorities.[94]

10. Technology and innovation

Risks

Promoting and sharing technologies may contribute to create an environment that supports the enjoyment of human rights and enhance environmental protection. However, empirical studies suggest that actual technology transfer in the agricultural sector is seldom up to the level announced by enterprises (UNCTAD, 2009).

As regards genetic material and the traditional knowledge of indigenous peoples, local communities and farmers, States Parties to the CBD, the International Treaty on Plant Genetic Resources for Food and Agriculture and the Nagoya Protocol on Access and Benefit-sharing to the CBD, have specific international obligations related to access to genetic resources and associated traditional knowledge. Enterprises may collaborate with governments to support them in complying with these international obligations, or at the very least not undermine them, taking into account relevant intellectual property laws.

Risk mitigation measures

- Endeavour to ensure that activities are compatible with the science and technology policies and plans of **host countries** and, as appropriate, contribute to the development of local and national innovative capacity.

- Adopt, where practicable in the course of the operations, practices that permit the **transfer and rapid diffusion** of locally-adapted and innovative technologies, know-how and practices, with due regard to the protection of intellectual property rights.[95]

- Subject to national law and in accordance with applicable international treaties, respect the **right of farmers** to save, use, exchange and sell genetic resources, including seeds, and recognise the interests of breeders.[96]

- When appropriate, perform science and technology development work in developing countries that aim to address **local market** needs, employ local personnel and encourage their training, taking into account commercial needs.

- When granting licenses for the use of **intellectual property rights** or when otherwise transferring technology, do so on reasonable terms and conditions and in a manner that contributes to the long term sustainable development of the host country.

- Where relevant to commercial objectives, develop ties with **local universities**, public research institutions, and participate in co-operative research projects with local industry or industry associations.[97]

Annex A Notes

1. OECD Guidelines, III.1-3, VIII.2; CFS-RAI Principle 9.ii; VGGT, 12.3; Akwé: Kon Guidelines, 10-11; IFC Performance Standard 1, 29; UN Principles for Responsible Contracts appended to the UN Guiding Principles and endorsed by the UN Human Rights Council, Principle 10. This may also support the implementation of the Aarhus Convention, Article 5.6. Information on the *'characteristics of products'* should include information that is sufficient to enable consumers to make informed decisions, including information on the prices and, where appropriate, content, safe use, environmental attributes, maintenance, storage and disposal of products (MNE Guidelines, VIII.2).
2. Akwé: Kon Guidelines, 10-11.
3. Aarhus Convention, Article 5.1.c.
4. OECD Guidelines, III.1.
5. IFC Performance Standard 1, para. 27.
6. IFC Performance Standard 7, paras. 13-17; Akwé: Kon Guidelines, 29, 52-53, 60; VGGT, 3B.6, 9.9; CFS-RAI Principle 9.iii; UN Declaration on the Rights of Indigenous Peoples, Article 10. As per IFC Performance Standard 1, para 33, where stakeholder engagement is primarily the responsibility of the government, enterprises should collaborate with the responsible government agency, to the extent permitted by the agency. Where government capacity is limited, they should play an active role during the stakeholder engagement planning, implementation, and monitoring. If the process conducted by the government does not meet the relevant requirements for meaningful engagement, they should conduct a complementary process and, where appropriate, identify supplemental actions.
7. VGGT, 3B.6; IFC Performance Standard 1, 30.
8. VGGT, 9.9 and 4.10; Akwé: Kon Guidelines, 14-17; PRAI Principles 1 and 4; IFC Performance Standard 1, 26-27 and 30.
9. Akwé: Kon Guidelines, 17; IFC Performance Standard 1, 30-31.
10. Akwé: Kon Guidelines, 7-8; IFC Performance Standard 1, 27.
11. OECD Guidelines, VI.3 and VI.67.
12. Tools such as High Conservation Value and Carbon Stock Assessments can be used. You can refer to sub-section 8 on 'environmental protection and sustainable use of natural resources' for further details on potential adverse environmental impacts.
13. CFS-RAI Principle 10; Akwé: Kon Guidelines, 6, 37 and 48.
14. CFS-RAI Principle 10.i; Akwé: Kon Guidelines, 14.
15. IFC Performance Standard 1, paras 8 and 10.
16. CBD Articles 8(j) and 10; ITPGR Article 9.2; Nagoya Protocol Article 5; ILO Convention 169, Article 15.
17. An indicative list can be found in the Annex to the Nagoya Protocol.
18. Akwé: Kon Guidelines, 46.

19. CFS-RAI Principles 1.iii and 2, iv-vii; PRAI Principle 6; ILO MNE Declaration, para. 20; Akwé: Kon Guidelines, 46; IFC Performance Standard 7, paras 18-20.

20. ILO MNE Declaration, para. 10, PRAI Principle 5.

21. PRAI Principle 6; Akwé Kon Guidelines, 46; IFC Performance Standard 7, paras 18-20.

22. IFC Performance Standard 1, para 35.

23. UN Guiding Principle 31, commentary.

24. OECD Guidelines, IV.46.

25. OECD Guidelines, IV.1-3.

26. OECD Guidelines, IV.37.

27. Akwé: Kon Guidelines 13; IFC Performance Standard 7, para.8.

28. See the section above on impact assessments for more details.

29. OECD Guidelines, II.2 and IV.5 and 45.

30. CFS-RAI Principles 3 and 4.

31. CFS-RAI Principle 3; Convention on the Elimination of All Forms of Discrimination Against Women (CEDAW).

32. CFS-RAI Principle 3.iii.

33. Freedom of Association and Protection of the Right to Organise Convention, 1948 (No. 87); Right to Organise and Collective Bargaining Convention, 1949 (No. 98); Forced Labour Convention, 1930 (No. 29); Abolition of Forced Labour Convention, 1957 (No. 105); Minimum Age Convention, 1973 (No. 138); Worst Forms of Child Labour Convention, 1999 (No. 182); Equal Remuneration Convention, 1951 (No. 100); Discrimination (Employment and Occupation) Convention, 1958 (No. 111).

34. In addition, the right to join and form trades unions is protected by the European Convention on Human Rights (Article 11). The right to join trade unions is protected by the right to freedom of association contained in the American Convention on Human Rights (Article 16) and the African Charter on Human and Peoples' Rights (Article 10).

35. CFS-RAI Principle 2 covers labour rights.

36. ILO MNE Declaration 21; OECD Guidelines, V.1.e. Commentary 54 of the OECD Guidelines specifies that the term "other status" for the purposes of the Guidelines refers to trade union activity and personal characteristics such as age, disability, pregnancy, marital status, sexual orientation, or HIV status. It is worth noting that the Convention on the Rights of Persons with Disabilities (CRPD) prohibits discrimination in employment on the basis of disability.

37. ILO MNE Declaration 36; OECD Guidelines, V.1.c; Children's Rights and Business Principle 2. The Children's Rights and Business Principles do not create new international legal obligations. They are founded on the rights outlined in the Convention on the Rights of the Child and its Optional Protocols. The Convention is the most widely ratified human rights treaty: 193 governments have signed and ratified the Convention. These Principles are also based on the ILO Conventions No. 182 on the Worst Forms of Child Labour and No. 138 on the Minimum Age. They

also elaborate on existing standards for business, including the UN Global Compact's 'Ten Principles' and the UN Guiding Principles.

38. OECD Guidelines, V.1.d; IFC Performance Standard 2, paras. 13, 15, 21, 22 and 27.

39. ILO MNE Declaration, 34; OECD Guidelines, V.4.a & b.

40. ILO MNE Declaration, 25.

41. ILO MNE Declaration, 26; OECD Guidelines, V.6.

42. ILO Communications within the Undertaking Recommendation, 1967 (No. 129), para. 2.

43. Industrial relations systems, including collective bargaining at company and sector levels, can play an important role in preventing and addressing grievances.

44. IFC Performance Standard 2, 14; ILO MNE Declaration, 17, 52-53.

45. OECD Guidelines, II.9, V.1-3, V.6-8; ILO MNE Declaration, 41, 44, 47, 51-56.

46. OECD Guidelines, V.4-5; ILO MNE Declaration, para. 18.

47. ILO MNE Declaration, 16-18, 30-34.

48. CFS-RAI Principles 3.iii and 4.ii.

49. ILO MNE Declaration, 31.

50. The following countries and organisations have endorsed this approach: European Commission, US Department of State, US Department of Agriculture, US Centre for Disease Control and Prevention (CDC), World Bank, World Health Organization (WHO), FAO, OIE, and United Nations System Influenza Coordination (UNSIC). For further information, consult www.onehealthglobal.net.

51. The General Comments of the Committee on Economic, Social and Cultural Rights are non-binding but authoritative interpretations of the ICESCR.

52. Committee on Economic, Social and Cultural Rights, General Comment No. 14 of 2000. Though the ICESCR is a widely-ratified international instrument in which States Parties recognise the right to the enjoyment of the highest attainable standard of physical and mental health, health-related rights are also found in other instruments, including the Convention on the Rights of the Child (CRC), the Convention on the Elimination of all Forms of Discrimination against Women (CEDAW), the Convention on the Elimination of All Forms of Racial Discrimination (CERD), and the Convention on the Rights of Persons with Disabilities (CRPD).

53. For specific recommendations on consumer interests, see the OECD Guidelines, VIII.

54. The IFC Performance Standard 3 defines 'good international practice' as 'the exercise of professional skill, diligence, prudence, and foresight that would reasonably be expected from skilled and experienced professionals engaged in the same type of undertaking under the same or similar circumstances globally or regionally. The outcome of such exercise should be that the project employs the most appropriate technologies in the project-specific circumstances'.

55. IFC Performance Standard 4.

56. PRAI Principle 5. The Codex Alimentarius Commission, established by FAO and the World Health Organization (WHO) in 1963, proposes international food standards, guidelines and codes of practice to protect the health of the consumers and ensure fair

practices in food trade. The Commission also promotes the co-ordination among various food standards developed by international governmental and non-governmental organisations. HACCP principles are part of the Codex. They are a systematic preventive approach to food safety and biological, chemical, and physical hazards in production processes that can cause the finished product to be unsafe. They design measurements to reduce these risks to a safe level. The seven principles are as follows: (1) conduct a hazard analysis; (2) identify the critical control points; (3) establish critical limits; (4) monitor the critical control points; (5) establish corrective action; (6) verify; and (7) keep records. The HACCP system can be used at all stages of a food chain, from food production and preparation processes, including packaging and distribution.

57. For instance, schemes recognised by the Global Food Safety Initiative include the SSC 22000 Food Safety Management System and BRC Global Standards and International Featured Standards. The European Food Safety Authority also provides food safety standards.

58. As per the Codex Alimentarius Commission of 2006, traceability is defined as the ability to follow the movement of food through specified stages of production, processing and distribution. The traceability tool should be able to identify at any specified stage of the food supply chain from where the food came (one step back) and to where the food went (one step forward), as appropriate to the objectives of the food inspection and certification system.

59. Food-related rights are also protected in other international and regional instruments, including the Convention on the Rights of the Child (CRC), the Convention on the Elimination of all Forms of Discrimination against Women (CEDAW), and the Convention on the Rights of Persons with Disabilities (CRPD).

60. UN Committee on Economic, Social and Cultural Rights, General Comment 12 (1999), paras. 6, 15 and 27.

61. For further information, refer to the Access to Nutrition Index at www.accesstonutrition.org.

62. CFS-RAI Principles 1.i and iii, 2.iii and iv, and 8.i; 3.i and iii; VGGT, 12.4; PRAI Principle 2.

63. The CAO is the independent recourse mechanism for the IFC and the Multilateral Investment Guarantee Agency (MIGA). It responds to complaints from project-affected communities with the goal of enhancing social and environmental outcomes on the ground.

64. Although tenure rights over land and other natural resources are not human rights, they may have important implications for the enjoyment of various human rights and are reflected in RBC standards. One important exception is the right of indigenous peoples to ownership and possession over lands they traditionally occupy, which is codified in ILO Convention 169 and promoted in the non-binding but widely cited UN Declaration on the Rights of Indigenous Peoples (see Annex B).

65. Involuntary resettlement refers both to physical displacement (relocation from or loss of land) and economic displacement (loss of natural resources or diminished access to natural resources that leads to loss of livelihood) as a result of land acquisition and/or restrictions on natural resource use. Resettlement is considered involuntary when

affected persons do not have the right to refuse land acquisition and/or restrictions on natural resource use (IFC Performance Standard 5).

66. VGGT, 2.4; PRAI Principle 1; Akwé: Kon Guidelines 13; IFC Performance Standard 7, para 8.

67. Akwé: Kon Guidelines 13.

68. VGGT, 12.4 and 16.1; IFC Performance Standard 5, para 8; ILO Convention on Indigenous and Tribal Peoples, 1989 (No. 169), Article 16. Note that these standards are also referred to in the recent commitments of major agri-food companies on land grabbing.

69. PRAI, 6.2.1; IFC Performance Standard 5, paras. 9-10, 19, 27-28, and IFC Performance Standard 7, paras 9 and 14.

70. IFC Performance Standard 5, para. 30. In addition, paragraph 31 of this standard requires enterprises to prepare a supplemental resettlement and livelihood restoration plan.

71. According to the OIE's definition recognised by more than 170 countries, animal welfare means how an animal is coping with the conditions in which it lives. An animal is in a good state of welfare if (as indicated by scientific evidence) it is healthy, comfortable, well nourished, safe, able to express innate behaviour, and if it is not suffering from unpleasant states such as pain, fear and distress. For further information, see *www.defra.gov.uk/fawc*.

72. The five freedoms are acknowledged in the introduction of OIE's recommendations on Animal Welfare, i.e. in Article 7.1.2. of the Terrestrial Animal Health Code. For further information, see the Farm Animal Welfare Council's Five Freedoms at *www.fawc.org.uk/freedoms.htm*.

73. See *http://eur-lex.europa.eu/legal-content/EN/TXT/?uri=CELEX:12012E/TXT*.

74. These standards include: IFC Good Practice Note on Animal Welfare in Livestock Operations; Freedom Food of the Royal Society for the Prevention of Cruelty to Animals (RSPCA); Label Rouge; GAP 5-step; and the Soil Association's organic standards.

75. OIE, Terrestrial Animal Health Code 2015, Article 7.1.4. These risk mitigation measures appear in line with the substantive criteria of the Business Benchmark on Farm Animal Welfare (*www.bbfaw.com*).

76. A pest management plan should aim to reduce pest development by combining various techniques, such as biological control by using beneficial insects or microbes, pest-resistant crop varieties and alternative agricultural practices such as spraying or pruning.

77. OECD Guidelines, VI.1.

78. IFC Performance Standard 1, paras 5 and 21-22.

79. OECD Guidelines, VI.2-3.

80. OECD Guidelines, VI.1, 4-5; IFC Performance Standard 1, 5 and 21-22; UN Global Compact, Principles 7-8; United Nations Framework Convention on Climate Change, Article 3.

81. OECD Guidelines, VI.1, 4, and 5; IFC Performance Standard 1, paras. 5 and 21-22.

82. OECD Guidelines, VI.2-3.

83. IFC Performance Standard 6, para. 7; CBD Articles 8 and 9; CFS-RAI Principle 6.ii. IFC Performance Standard 6, para 26, also states that 'Where feasible, the client will locate land-based agribusiness and forestry projects on unforested land or land already converted'. The Forest Policy Proposals of the International Commission on Land Use Change and Ecosystems (October 2009), the EU Renewable Energy Directive No. 2009/28/EG (April 2009), the EU Timber Regulation No. 995/2010 (October 2010), and the New York Declaration on Forests adopted at the Climate Summit 2014, refer to land use changes.

84. PRAI Principle 7. For example, soil fertility can be preserved through appropriate crop rotations, manure application, pasture management and rational mechanical or conservation tillage practices.

85. The CEO Water Mandate - a public-private initiative launched by the UN Secretary-General in 2007 designed to assist companies in developing, implementing and disclosing water sustainability policies and practices - requires setting targets related to water conservation, waste-water treatment and the reduction of water consumption. However, Rio +20 outcome document 'The Future We Want' rather focuses on increasing water use efficiency and reducing water losses.

86. CFS-RAI Principle 8.iii.

87. CFS-RAI Principle 6.iii. Food waste should also be assessed, including by measuring it. Whenever feasible, waste should be minimised, for instance by transferring technology to third parties or raising awareness on food waste and its consequences. When waste cannot be avoided, food sent to landfills should be minimised by, for instance, using it for animal feed or transforming it into energy when appropriate.

88. IFC Performance Standard 3.6.

89. CFS-RAI Principle 6.v.

90. OECD Guidelines, II.A.5 & 15, and VII.

91. VGGT, 6.9, 8.9, 9.12, 16.6, 17.5.

92. For further details on how states can take effective measures to deter, prevent and combat the bribery of foreign public officials in connection with international business transactions, see the OECD Recommendation of the Council for Further Combating Bribery of Foreign Public Officials in International Business Transactions, *www.oecd.org/daf/anti-bribery/44176910.pdf.*

93. OECD Guidelines, XI.1-2.

94. OECD Guidelines, X.2-3.

95. OECD Guidelines, IX.1-2 ; CFS-RAI Principle 7.iv.

96. CFS-RAI Principle 7.ii; International Treaty on Plant Genetic Resources for Food and Agriculture, Article 9.3.

97. OECD Guidelines, IX.

Annex A References

CAO (2013), *Annual Report*, Compliance Advisor Ombudsman, Washington DC.

CAO (2008), A Guide to Designing and Implementing Grievance Mechanisms for Development Projects, Advisory Note, Compliance Advisor Ombudsman, Washington DC.

DEFRA (2003), "Preface", in *The Code of Recommendations for the Welfare of Livestock*, United Kingdom Department of Environment, Food and Rural Affairs, London.

EC (2011), *Report - A Sectoral Approach to CSR to Tackle Societal Issues in the Food Supply Chain*, High Level Forum for a Better Functioning Food Supply Chain, Expert Platform on the Competitiveness of the Agro-food Industry, European Commission, Brussels.

FAO (2013), Trends and Impacts of Foreign Agricultural Investment in Developing Country Agriculture: Evidence from Case Studies, Food and Agriculture Organization, Rome.

FAO (2011), Report of Expert Meeting on International Investment in the Agricultural Sector of Developing Countries, 22-23 November 2011, Food and Agriculture Organization, Rome.

FAO (2010), *Principles for Responsible Agricultural Investment that Respects Rights, Livelihoods and Resources*, Discussion Note Prepared by FAO, IFAD, UNCTAD and the World Bank Group, Food and Agriculture Organization, Rome.

IFC (2014), *Improving Animal Welfare in Livestock Operations*, Good Practice Note, International Finance Corporation, Washington DC.

IFC (2012), *IFC Performance Standards*, International Finance Corporation, Washington DC.

IFC (2009), Addressing Grievances from Project-affected Communities - Guide for Projects and Companies Designing Grievance Mechanisms, Good Practice Note No. 7, International Finance Corporation, Washington DC.

IFPRI (2006), Occupational Health Hazards of Agriculture - Understanding the Links between Agriculture and Health, Brief 13(8), International Food Policy Research Institute, Washington DC.

ILO (2011a), "Unleashing rural development through productive employment and decent work: Building on 40 years of ILO work in rural areas", *Paper to the Governing Body's Committee on Employment and Social Policy*, International Labour Organization, Geneva.

ILO (2011b), *Safety and Health in Agriculture, Code of Practice*, International Labour Organization, Geneva.

ILO (2008), The Labour Principles of the United Nations Global Compact: A Guide for Business, International Labour Organization, Geneva.

ILO (2006), Tripartite Declaration of Principles concerning Multinational Enterprises and Social Policy, International Labour Organization, Geneva.

ILO (2005), *Safety and Health in Agriculture*, International Labour Organization, Geneva.

McDermott, M. *et al.* (2015), *Towards the Valuation of Unregistered Land*, Paper Prepared for a Presentation at the 2015 World Bank Conference on Land and Poverty by McDermott, M., Selebalo, C. and Boydell, S., World Bank, Washington DC.

Munden Project (2013), Global Capital, Local Concessions: A Data-Driven Examination of Land Tenure Risk and Industrial Concessions in Emerging Market Economies, The Munden Project Ltd.

OECD (2011), *OECD Guidelines for Multinational Enterprises, 2011 Edition*, OECD Publishing, Paris. http://dx.doi.org/10.1787/9789264115415-en.

OECD (2006), "OECD Risk Awareness Tool for Multinational Enterprises in Weak Governance Zones", in *Annual Report on the OECD Guidelines for Multinational Enterprises 2006: Conducting Business in Weak Governance Zones*, OECD Publishing, Paris. http://dx.doi.org/10.1787/mne-2006-4-en.

RSPCA (2014), *Large-scale Farming, A Briefing Paper with an Emphasis on Dairy Farming*, Royal Society for the Prevention of Cruelty to Animals, Southwater.

TI (2011), "Corruption in the land sector", Working Paper 04/2011, Transparency International.

UN (2009), *Large-scale land acquisitions and leases - A set of minimum principles and measures to address the human rights challenge*, UN Special Rapporteur on the Right to Food, United Nations document A/HRC/13/33/3/Add.2, www.srfood.org/images/stories/pdf/officialreports/20100305_a-hrc-13-33-add2_land-principles_en.pdf.

UNCTAD (2009), *Transnational Corporations, Agricultural Production and Development*, World Investment Report, United Nations Conference on Trade and Development, New York and Geneva.

UNEP (2015), Bank and Investor Risk Policies on Soft Commodities, A Framework to Evaluate Deforestation and Forest Degradation Risk in the Agricultural Value Chain, United Nations Environment Programme.

UN HABITAT (2015), *Issue Papers and Policy Units of the Habitat III Conference*, United Nations Conference on Housing and Sustainable Urban Development, Nairobi.

WB and UNCTAD (2014), The Practice of Responsible Investment in Larger-Scale Agricultural Investments – Implications for Corporate Performance and Impacts on Local Communities, World Bank Report Number 86175-GLB, Agriculture and Environmental Services Discussion Paper 08, World Bank and United Nations Conference on Trade and Development, Washington DC.

Annex B

Engagement with indigenous peoples

As stated in the model enterprise policy, good-faith, effective and meaningful consultations with communities should be undertaken before initiating any operations that may affect them as well as during and at the end of operations. In addition, some international instruments and standards express a state commitment to engage in consultation in order to obtain the free prior and informed consent (FPIC) of indigenous peoples prior to the approval of any project affecting their lands or territories and other resources.[1] According to some human rights bodies and indigenous peoples, the concept of FPIC is derived from indigenous peoples' self-governance, territorial and cultural rights and is necessary for the realisation of those rights. Some countries have national laws consistent with a commitment to consult and co-operate to obtain FPIC.[2]

The CFS-RAI Principles and the VGGT call for meaningful consultations in order to obtain the FPIC of indigenous peoples. In addition, some major agri-food companies and commodity roundtables require obtaining FPIC in certain conditions. For instance, the Round Table on Sustainable Palm Oil (RSPO) requires the FPIC of affected groups for using land for palm oil plantations.[3] The OECD Guidelines make reference to UN instruments on the rights of indigenous peoples in the context of adverse human rights impacts but do not include any language on FPIC.[4]

Definition of indigenous peoples

There is no single definition of indigenous peoples, and indigenous groups are not homogenous entities. However, the International Labour Organization (ILO), drawing from its Convention No. 169, has characterised indigenous peoples as a distinct social and cultural group possessing the following characteristics in varying degrees:

- self-identification as members of a distinct cultural group
- traditional life styles
- culture and way of life different from the other segments of the national population, e.g. in their ways of making a living, language, customs, etc.
- own social organisation that may include traditional customs and/or laws.[5]

Self-identification as indigenous should be regarded as a fundamental criterion for determining indigenous peoples.[6]

Indigenous peoples may experience adverse impacts differently or more severely than other stakeholder groups, based on their relationship to the land that often plays a major role in social, cultural and religious practices, their culture and their socio-economic status. They are often among the most marginalised and vulnerable segments of the population. They may face discrimination and experience high poverty levels, thereby being more vulnerable and less resilient to adverse impacts. Regardless of the legal framework in which an operation takes place, they often have customary or traditional rights based on their relationship to the land, their culture and socio-economic status:

- **Land:** Indigenous peoples often have a special connection and/or customary rights to ancestral lands. This relationship to land is a distinguishing feature of indigenous peoples and therefore impacts related to land such as reduced or loss of access to land, or environmental degradation, may affect indigenous peoples, their livelihoods and culture, more severely than other, non-indigenous stakeholder groups. Furthermore, the customary land rights of indigenous people may not be recognised by national laws. Consultation should explore intangible value associated with sacred sites or areas of cultural significance.

- **Culture**: Indigenous peoples may hold unique cultural values and characteristics which should be considered and respected when engaging with them. For example, issues of privacy can be of particular importance to indigenous peoples, e.g. due to a legacy of social or cultural discrimination and marginalisation, or sensitivity due to a lack of contact with mainstream cultures. In such instances, appropriate engagement practice could include seeking consent when recording information about rituals, ceremonies and rites of passage to ensure against disruption of cultural life. This is particularly important when the operations result in resettlement and/or displacement. Given that indigenous peoples' traditional way of life is usually intimately linked with a specific territory, resettlement may lead to a loss of social networks, cultural erosion, and loss of language and distinct identity. Employment in large-scale business activities may likewise be seen as a detriment to traditional activities by some indigenous peoples. The introduction of a cash economy may be incompatible with previously-existing relationships of exchange. Engagement with indigenous peoples can identify ways to mitigate these impacts and reflect their aspirations and priorities.

- **Socio-economic status:** In many parts of the world, indigenous peoples are among the most marginalised and vulnerable segments of the population. They often face discrimination and experience high levels of poverty and social disadvantage. Often, they are less informed about and less able to defend their rights and cultural heritage. This means that they may be less resilient to shocks and adverse impacts and more vulnerable to serious economic and social consequences. They may speak unique dialects or rely on oral tradition for communicating information which can lead to difficulties in effectively communicating information, and may require innovative methods of consultation and engagement. Additionally it is important to consider that historical grievances may exist and could complicate activities.

Indigenous groups comprise individuals who experience adverse impacts differently and include more vulnerable groups, such as women and children, with whom special attention during the engagement process would be expected.

Implementing FPIC

Enterprises should always obey domestic laws and regulations as well as respect relevant internationally recognised human rights.[7] Irrespective of regulatory or operational requirements and throughout their project planning, they should anticipate that indigenous peoples may expect consultation seeking FPIC and that risks may be generated if such expectations are not met. In countries where FPIC is not mandated, enterprises should consider local expectations, the risks posed to indigenous peoples[8] and to the operations as a result of local opposition. They should pursue an engagement strategy that meets the legitimate expectations of indigenous peoples to the extent that they do not violate domestic law.

In this regard, the following key steps may be useful to engage with indigenous peoples when seeking to implement FPIC:

- Agree with affected indigenous peoples on a consultation process for working towards seeking FPIC. This should identify the specific current and future activities where consent should be sought.[9] In some cases it might be appropriate to commit to this process through a formal or legal agreement.[10] The process should always be based on good faith negotiation free of coercion, intimidation or manipulation.

- Consult and agree on what constitutes appropriate consent for affected indigenous peoples in accordance with their governance institutions, customary laws and practices, e.g. whether this is a majority vote from the community or approval of the council of elders. Indigenous peoples should be able to participate through their own freely chosen representatives and customary or other institutions.

- Engage in the process of seeking consent as soon as possible during project planning, before activities for which consent should be sought for commence or are authorised.

- Recognise the process of seeking FPIC as iterative rather than a one-off discussion. Continuous dialogue with the local community will lead to a trust relationship and a balanced agreement that will benefit the investment across all phases of the project.

- Provide all information relating to the activity to indigenous communities in a manner that is timely, objective, accurate and understandable to them.

- Document commitments/agreements that have been reached, including, as relevant, specification of what activities consent has been granted for or withheld, any conditions of consent, and areas of ongoing negotiation and share them with the indigenous community in a form and language they can understand and in a timely manner.

- Determine what action(s) will be taken in the event that: a) indigenous peoples refuse to enter into negotiations; and b) indigenous peoples do not give their consent for activities in their territory.

Responding to a lack of consent or refusal to engage

When consent is withheld by an indigenous community, an enterprise should consult with the community to understand the reasons behind the lack of consent and whether ongoing concerns can be addressed or accommodated. Consent previously granted under free, prior and informed conditions should not be withdrawn arbitrarily.

In cases where consent is not forthcoming or where indigenous peoples refuse to engage, material risks to the enterprise and adverse impacts to indigenous peoples may be generated. In situations where proceeding with projects will cause adverse impacts to indigenous peoples, an enterprise should take the necessary steps to cease or prevent such impacts.[11]

If, through its due diligence,[12] an enterprise concludes that consent is required to proceed with an activity, and the agreed process has not arrived at consent, activities should not proceed unless FPIC is subsequently forthcoming. For example, a project financed by IFC should not proceed, regardless of any authorisation by the state, if relocation of indigenous populations is required and if FPIC has not been obtained from them.

Excerpts from existing instruments and standards

Standard	FPIC-related text
UN Declaration on the Rights of Indigenous Peoples (UNDRIP)*	*No relocation shall take place without the FPIC of the indigenous peoples concerned (Article 10).* *States shall provide redress through effective mechanisms, which may include restitution, developed in conjunction with indigenous peoples, with respect to their cultural, intellectual, religious and spiritual property taken without their FPIC or in violation of their laws, traditions and customs (Article 11).* *States shall consult and cooperate in good faith with the indigenous peoples concerned through their own representative institutions in order to obtain their FPIC prior to the approval of any project affecting their lands or territories and other resources, particularly in connection with the development, utilization or exploitation of mineral, water and other resources (Article 32).* Additional references to FPIC are included in Articles 19, 29 and 30.
ILO Convention No. 169 on Indigenous and Tribal Peoples**	*Where the relocation of these peoples is considered necessary as an exceptional measure, such relocation shall take place only with their free and informed consent. Where their consent cannot be obtained, such relocation shall take place only following appropriate procedures established by national laws and regulations, including public inquiries where appropriate, which provide the opportunity for effective representation of the peoples concerned (Article 16).*
CFS-RAI Principles	*Responsible investment in agriculture and food systems should...incorporate inclusive and transparent governance structures, processes, decision-making...through... effective and meaningful*

Standard	FPIC-related text
	consultation with indigenous peoples, through their representative institutions in order to obtain their FPIC under the United Nations Declaration of Rights of Indigenous Peoples and with due regard for particular positions and understanding of individual States (Principle 9).
VGGT	*States and other parties should hold good faith consultation with indigenous peoples before initiating any project or before adopting and implementing legislative or administrative measures affecting the resources for which the communities hold rights. Such projects should be based on an effective and meaningful consultation with indigenous peoples, through their own representative institutions in order to obtain their FPIC under the United Nations Declaration of Rights of Indigenous Peoples and with due regard for particular positions and understandings of individual States (Para 9.9).* *In the case of indigenous peoples and their communities, States should ensure that all actions are consistent with their existing obligations under national and international law, and with due regard to voluntary commitments under applicable regional and international instruments, including as appropriate from the ILO Convention No. 169 concerning Indigenous and Tribal Peoples in Independent Countries and the UN Declaration on the Rights of Indigenous Peoples (Para 12.7).*
Akwe: Kon Guidelines	*In the conduct of cultural impact assessments, due consideration should be given to the holders of traditional knowledge, innovations and practices and the knowledge itself... In the event of the disclosure of secret and or sacred knowledge, prior informed consent and proper protection measures should be ensured (Para 29).* *The following general considerations should also be taken into account when carrying out an impact assessment for a development proposed to take place on, or which is likely to impact on, sacred sites and on lands and waters traditionally occupied or used by indigenous and local communities:* • *Prior informed consent of the affected indigenous and local communities: Where the national legal regime requires prior informed consent of indigenous and local communities, the assessment process should consider whether such prior informed consent has been obtained. Prior informed consent corresponding to various phases of the impact assessment process should consider the rights, knowledge, innovations and practices of indigenous and local communities; the use of appropriate language and process; the allocation of sufficient time and the provision of accurate, factual and legally correct information. Modifications to the initial development proposal will require the additional prior informed consent of the affected indigenous and local communities (Para 53).* • *Ownership, protection and control of traditional knowledge, innovations and practices and technologies used in cultural,*

Standard	FPIC-related text
	environmental and social impact assessment processes... Such knowledge should only be used with the prior informed consent of the owners of that traditional knowledge (Para 60).
IFC Performance Standards	*There is no universally accepted definition of FPIC (...). FPIC builds on and expands the process of Informed Consultation and Participation described in Performance Standard 1 and will be established through good faith negotiation between the client and the Affected Communities of Indigenous Peoples. The client will document: (i) the mutually accepted process between the client and Affected Communities of Indigenous Peoples, and (ii) evidence of agreement between the parties as the outcome of the negotiations. FPIC does not necessarily require unanimity and may be achieved even when individuals or groups within the community explicitly disagree.* *Affected communities of indigenous peoples may be particularly vulnerable to the loss of, alienation from or exploitation of their land and access to natural and cultural resources. In recognition of this vulnerability, the client will obtain the FPIC of the affected communities of indigenous peoples in the following circumstances:* • *Impacts on lands and natural resources subject to traditional ownership or under customary use.* • *Relocation of indigenous peoples from lands and natural resources subject to traditional ownership or under customary use: The client will consider feasible alternative project designs to avoid the relocation of indigenous peoples from communally held lands and natural resources subject to traditional ownership or under customary use. If such relocation is unavoidable the client will not proceed with the project unless FPIC has been obtained.* • *Critical cultural heritage: Where significant project impacts on critical cultural heritage are unavoidable, the client will obtain the FPIC of the affected communities of indigenous peoples. Where a project proposes to use the cultural heritage including knowledge, innovations, or practices of indigenous peoples for commercial purposes, the client will...obtain the FPIC of the affected communities of indigenous peoples.*

* The 2007 Declaration is a non-legally binding document that has been adopted by the UN General Assembly with 143 countries in favour, 4 against and 11 abstaining. It represents their political intention.

** This Convention of 1989 is binding on the 22 countries that have ratified it. Its adoption within ILO represents a consensus among ILO tripartite constituents about the rights of indigenous and tribal peoples and the responsibilities of governments to protect these rights. The foundations of the Convention are: respect for the cultures and way of life of indigenous peoples, recognition of their right to land and natural resources, and their right to define their own priorities for development. Its key principles are consultation and participation.

For further guidance on FPIC

Expert Mechanism on the Rights of Indigenous Peoples (2011), Expert Mechanism advice No. 2: indigenous peoples and the right to participate in decision-making. Geneva.

Foley-Hoag (2010), Implementing a corporate free, prior, and informed consent policy: benefits and challenges, by Lehr, A. and Smith, G. *www.foleyhoag.com/publications/ebooks-and-white-papers/2010/may/implementing-a-corporate-free-prior-and-informed-consent-policy*.

FAO (2014), Respecting free, prior and informed consent - Practical guidance for governments, companies, NGOs, indigenous peoples and local communities in relation to land acquisition, Governance of tenure technical guide 3.

ILO (2013), Understanding the Indigenous and Tribal Peoples Convention, 1989 (No.169), Handbook for ILO Tripartite Constituents, International Labour Standards Department, International Labour Organisation, Geneva.

OECD (2016), *OECD Due Diligence Guidance for Meaningful Stakeholder Engagement in the Extractive Sector*, forthcoming, OECD Publishing, Paris.

Oxfam Australia (2005), Guide to free, prior and informed consent, by Hill, C., Lillywhite, S. and Simon, S., Carlton, Victoria, Australia.

RSB (2011), RSB guidelines for land rights: respecting rights, identifying risks, avoiding and resolving disputes and acquiring lands through free, prior and informed consent, Roundtable on Sustainable Biofuels, Geneva.

UN Permanent Forum on Indigenous Issues (2005), Report of the International Workshop on Methodologies Regarding Free, Prior and Informed Consent and Indigenous Peoples. Document E/C.19/2005/3, submitted to the Fourth Session of the UNPFII, 16-17 May.

World Bank (2005), Operational Policy 4.10: Indigenous Peoples. Washington, DC.

Annex B Notes

1. The international instruments relating to indigenous peoples are UNDRIP and ILO Convention No. 169. UNDRIP recommends that states consult and co-operate with indigenous peoples concerned in order to obtain their FPIC in a number of situations, including for projects affecting their land and territories or other resources (Articles 19 and 32). ILO Convention No. 169, which is legally binding for countries that have ratified it, requires state parties to consult with indigenous peoples with the objective of reaching agreement or consent on proposed measures (Article 6). For guidance on the Convention's provision on consent, see ILO Handbook for ILO Tripartite Constituents – Understanding the Indigenous and Tribal Peoples Convention, 1989 (No. 169) (2013). Other UN bodies argue that international standards with regard to FPIC apply equally to non-state actors. These bodies include the UN Permanent Forum on Indigenous Issues, the UN Working Group on the issue of human rights and transnational corporations and other business enterprises, the UN Special Rapporteur on the rights of indigenous peoples, the UN Experts Mechanism on the Rights of Indigenous Peoples, and several UN Human Rights Treaty Bodies.

2. FAO, "Respecting free, prior and informed consent – practical guidance for governments, companies, NGOs, indigenous peoples and local communities in relation to land acquisition" (2014), p. 7, *www.fao.org/3/a-i3496e.pdf*.

3. The 'Principles and criteria for the production of sustainable palm oil' endorsed by the RSPO Executive Board and accepted at the Extraordinary General Assembly by RSPO members on 25 April 2013 state that the use of the land for oil palm does not diminish the legal, customary or user rights of other users without their free, prior and informed consent (Principle 2.3.). As an indicator, copies of negotiated agreements detailing the process of FPIC should be available and include: a) Evidence that a plan has been developed through consultation and discussion with all affected groups in the communities, and that information has been provided to all affected groups, including information on the steps that shall be taken to involve them in decision making; b) Evidence that the company has respected communities' decisions to give or withhold their consent to the operation at the time that this decision was taken; c) Evidence that the legal, economic, environmental and social implications for permitting operations on their land have been understood and accepted by affected communities, including the implications for the legal status of their land at the expiry of the company's title, concession or lease on the land.

4. See OECD Guidelines, IV.40: '[…]'enterprises should respect the human rights of individuals belonging to specific groups or populations that require particular attention, where they may have adverse human rights impacts on them. In this connection, UN instruments have elaborated further on the rights of indigenous peoples […].''

5. ILO Convention No. 169 sets forth the following definitions of indigenous and tribal peoples. *Tribal peoples:* their social, cultural and economic conditions distinguish them from other sections of the national community, and their status is regulated wholly or partially by their own customs or traditions or by special laws or regulations; *Indigenous peoples:* they are regarded as indigenous on account of their descent from the populations which inhabited the country or a geographical region to which the country belongs, at the time of conquest or colonisation or the

establishment of present state boundaries and who, irrespective of their legal status, retain some or all of their own social, economic, cultural and political institutions.

6. See ILO Convention No. 169, Article 1.2.

7. OECD Guidelines, I.2 and IV. 1.

8. The following resources provide details on communities' expectations in relation to FPIC: *Guide to Free Prior and Informed Consent,* http://resources.oxfam.org.au/pages/view.php?ref=588&search=mining&order_by=relevance&sort=DESC&offset=48&archive=0&k=&curpos=54, Oxfam Australia (2014); *Making Free Prior and Informed Consent a Reality: Indigenous Peoples and the Extractive Industries,* Doyle C. and Carino J., Middlesex University, PIPLinks & ECCR (2013), www.ecojesuit.com/wp-content/uploads/2014/09/Making-FPIC-a-Reality-Report.pdf.

9. The international instruments referred to in the table below specify the circumstances in which FPIC is relevant, for example in cases when resettlement is needed.

10. It has been suggested that FPIC can be understood as a heightened and more formalised form of community engagement. As a result, in certain cases companies may be motivated to enter into a more formal consultation process when developing a project on or near indigenous territory that may have significant adverse impacts. See Lehr & Smith, *Implementing a Corporate Free Prior Informed Consent Policy,* www.foleyhoag.com/publications/ebooks-and-white-papers/2010/may/implementing-a-corporate-free-prior-and-informed-consent-policy, Foley Hoag (2010), p. 8. The World Resources Institute advises companies trying to overcome the challenges of operationalising FPIC procedures through legal recognition of the process – ex. formal agreement, in combination with other good stakeholder engagement practices. See *Development without Conflict: The Business Case for Community Consent, Development without Conflict: The Business Case for Community Consent*, World Resources Institute (2007), http://webcache.googleusercontent.com/search?q=cache:KBxXOS9628IJ:pdf.wri.org/development_without_conflict_fpic.pdf+&cd=1&hl=en&ct=clnk&gl=fr.

11. OECD Guidelines, II.B.18-19 and IV.40 & 42.

12. Legal expertise should be sought to clarify legal obligations with regard to engagement with indigenous peoples.

OECD PUBLISHING, 2, rue André-Pascal, 75775 PARIS CEDEX 16
(20 2016 01 1 P) ISBN 978-92-64-25095-6 – 2016

www.ingramcontent.com/pod-product-compliance
Lightning Source LLC
LaVergne TN
LVHW080929120826
845149LV00018B/1800

9789264250956